Rudiments of Connoisseurship

BERNARD BERENSON

Rudiments of Connoisseurship

STUDY AND CRITICISM OF ITALIAN ART

SCHOCKEN BOOKS · NEW YORK

THE STUDY AND CRITICISM
OF ITALIAN ART   *   SECOND SERIES

First SCHOCKEN PAPERBACK edition 1962

Library of Congress Catalog Card No. 62-18157

Manufactured in the United States of America

PREFACE

In this volume there are but two papers which require explanation.

"A Word for Renaissance Churches" was written more than ten years ago, and published a year or two later. My excuse for reprinting it now is that so few writers, in English at least, have dealt with architecture from the point of view of the aesthetic spectator. Our books on architecture treat of this art in the first place from the builder's, and then from the religious person's standpoint, but, except by accident, never from any other. And yet one who is neither an architect, nor an antiquary, nor a churchman may look at a church; and, although he be none of these time-honoured personages, he nevertheless may enjoy the church with the acuteness of a physical sensation. He will carry the remembrance of it with him, and, reviving his emotion in tranquillity, will delve and delve until he fancies he has had a glimpse into the cause of his pleasure.

Being this kind of mere spectator, I spent happy years as a youth, wandering over the length and breadth of Italy. I saw a great deal; and, reduced frequently by the plain living of an Umbrian inn or Tuscan pothouse to seek for relief in study and

v

reflection, I would try to account to myself for my impressions. Nor was I left utterly unguided and uncounselled. There was a book that always went with me, or, to be more accurate, part of a book—the section on Architecture in Burckhardt's "Cicerone." Helped on by the excellent Burckhardt, I kept asking myself what it was that I, who took neither the builder's nor the churchman's interest in architecture, found to admire in Renaissance churches, until an answer loomed before me. A small part of this answer was embodied in the essay now reprinted. Crudely stated, undeveloped, and incomplete, it yet may have some interest for other aesthetic spectators, for whom—for whom only, if they but knew it—all the arts exist.

The "Rudiments of Connoisseurship" has never appeared before. It was written more than eight years ago, as the first section of a book on the Methods of Constructive Art Criticism. I regret now that I did not go on with this book, for which there was, and still is, great need. Instead of an abstract discourse on Method, I thought it wiser to exemplify method in a concrete instance, and wrote my "Lotto." Now, although this work, in a special introduction, in the introductory paragraphs to each chapter, and here and there throughout, speaks of Method, yet to my no small astonishment, not a single reviewer of either the first or second edition has made the slightest reference to the general theory on which the book is based. And yet, but for the general theory, I scarcely should have allowed a second edition of "Lotto" to appear; for I origin-

ally selected this painter more for his excellence as
an illustration in Method, than for his actual achievements, although they are considerable, as an artist.

Had this abstract work been written, the question
of Method would scarcely have passed unnoticed.
A discussion might have arisen that could not but
have had a happy influence on our much abused
studies.   As it is, the facility in reproducing works
of art has created a great demand for knowledge
regarding them.   The demand finds but few who are
really competent to satisfy it; but it is too ignorant
and therefore too indiscriminate to know what it
wants, still less whether the information offered is
probable or improbable, interesting or uninterest-
ing, the fruit of intelligent labour or of impudent
quackery.

But as my interests have carried me away from
questions of Method, I no longer entertain the hope
of continuing the book begun eight years ago: so
that I now print the fragment which was to have
formed but a small part of it.   It is the part, however, which might have proved of greatest interest,
for although it was to have been, in some respects,
the least important, it deals with the now popular,
even fashionable, subject of Connoisseurship.

What Connoisseurship exacts, I have tried to state
in the paper now presented to the public.   Connoisseurship itself is not a new thing.   It has existed
for thousands of years.   A new spirit, however, or
rather a new practice, was introduced by Morelli.
Unfortunately, that great inventor was so much of
a mere empiric, that he could say, "The connoisseur

should above all things have no bump of philosophy." The result of this consistently held attitude of his was that his method laid itself out to ridicule, and, what is worse, misunderstanding. But Morelli's empiricism was founded on facts which, had he not deliberately refused to use his powers of reasoning, he easily could have thought out and stated, thus presenting himself, not as a mere happy inventor, but as a real discoverer. What he would not attempt, I have tried to do; and I dare believe that after perusing my essay the candid reader will no longer find anything ludicrous or trivial in the new Connoisseurship. It is my hope that this same essay will help to a better understanding, and to a better practice of this merely initial step in Constructive Art Criticism.

My thanks are due to the editors of the " Gazette des Beaux Arts," the " Revue Archéologique," the " American Journal of Archaeology," and Helbig's " Monatshefte," for the kind permission to reprint articles that they have published.

Florence,
  May, 1902.

CONTENTS

LIST OF ILLUSTRATIONS

xi

Rudiments of Connoisseurship

THE CAEN "SPOSALIZIO"

NOT a single opinion concerning the origin and the artistic development of Raphael has, in recent years, been allowed to pass unchallenged. The writers who occupy themselves with Italian Art, are arrayed in two camps, whose quarrels are as fierce as those of the Greeks and Trojans. Set battles or skirmishes —the warfare is for ever going on. One belief and one only has remained unassailed, as a palladium upon which neither Ulysses-Lermolieff nor Diomede-Minghetti has dared to lay a sacrilegious hand. Morellians and anti-Morellians, friends and enemies, are for once agreed about the influence exerted upon Raphael by Perugino's celebrated masterpiece, the "Sposalizio" of Caen. All are of a mind in recognizing that Raphael closely imitated this altarpiece in his own famous picture, painted originally for Città di Castello, and to-day the chief ornament of the Brera. "See how much Raphael owes to Perugino, in spite of the master's mediocrity and the pupil's incomparable genius," is murmured in the one camp—"Raphael's sun," the opposing faction replies, "did disappear for a time, it is true, behind the cloud of Perugino ; but it will presently shine forth again more resplendent than ever."

For my part, if my feeble voice could be heard, I

should say : Give over battle, for there is no cause
for strife.   If you will for a moment leave your
cries of defiance, and silence the drums and trumpets,
I shall try to show you that, in the first place, the
Caen " Sposalizio" was not painted by Perugino,
and, in the second, that in all likelihood it did *not
serve* as Raphael's model ; that it probably is nothing
but an imitation of this great painter's work.   If
you will have patience to listen to me, my arguments
will perhaps hasten the happy day, when we may
cease to fight about art, and begin to enjoy its calm
and tranquil pleasures.

I

When I went to Caen, I had not the shadow of a
doubt that I was going to see, not only one of
Perugino's best pictures, but certainly a picture
painted by him between the month of November,
1500—a date at which, as we know, the altar-piece
was not yet begun—and the year 1504, in the course
of which Raphael painted his admirable so-called
imitation.   Imagine my astonishment when, at the
first glance, the Caen picture presented me with
a combination of vivid colours, the like of which I
could not possibly recall in a single other work by
Perugino.   Only in two periods of his career, could
I remember works which even approached the
colouring in the picture before me, and these two
periods in no way coincided with the presumed date
of this work.   The one was at the very beginning
of his activity, as in his beautiful *tondo* in the
Louvre, and the other towards the end of his life, in
the numerous works he executed all over Umbria,
and of which the frescoes of S. Maria delle Lacrime

at Trevi are a good example. The very first glance, then, revealed to me the disconcerting fact that the "Sposalizio," supposing it were painted by Perugino, could not be a work of his middle career (his extreme youth being of course out of the question), that he could not, short of a miraculous leap, have painted it before 1504, and that it seemed most likely that it belonged to a much later date, which might reach even to 1515. A further examination led me to an even more unexpected conclusion, namely, that the excessive vivacity of the colour-scheme could not proceed from an artist whose taste, like Perugino's, had been chastened by the severe discipline of the Florentine school. In these gaudy hues there was a distinct note of provincialism which recalled some of the minor painters of the Veneto. Curiously enough, I observed a striking resemblance in colour between the famous picture of Caen, and a much more modest painting hung opposite to it, a rectangular *Pietà*, catalogued "Venetian School," but in reality by a Perugian artist of small fame, a certain Mariano di Ser Austerio.[1]

Such was my first impression of the Caen " Sposalizio." I will say no more for the moment about the colour, but I will insist upon several other important points. Among the most significant of these, must be counted the types, which, although clearly Umbrian, are not at all the types of Perugino. Another peculiarity is that the composition is framed in by two massive figures in profile, standing oppo-

[1] In this picture the Madonna is purely Peruginesque; the Dead Christ is the favourite type of the painter, as we find it in an authentic work—the *antipendium* in the Cambio Chapel at Perugia. The rather Venetian colouring, which is not habitual to him, may be due to his having made the acquaintance of Lotto in the Marches.

site to each other—a style of composition as rare in Perugino's works, as it is common in those of Pinturicchio, who makes use of it continually in his frescoes at Siena. The man of this balanced pair has in him absolutely nothing of Perugino : he is, on the contrary, entirely in Pinturicchio's tradition, with his fantastic head-dress and his right hand held out. This lay-figure, which we find with slight variations in the " Miracle of St. Bernardino," executed in 1473 by Fiorenzo di Lorenzo,[1] reappears continually in the works of his pupil Pinturicchio, as well in the earlier works, like the " Baptism " of the Sixtine Chapel, as in those of a later date, like the frescoes at Siena. This same figure in the " Sposalizio " gives us in an exaggerated form, a detail quite peculiar to Pinturicchio : the bent knees and bandy legs. The difficulty that the painter of the " Sposalizio " had in foreshortening the feet, and in balancing his figures in correct equilibrium, can be observed not only in this personage, but in almost all the other figures of the picture, and notably in those in the middle distance. Such strangely curved legs are not to be found anywhere in Perugino ; but they have their exact counterpart in the " Crowning of Æneas Sylvius as Poet" of Pinturicchio. Characteristic again, not of Perugino but of Pinturicchio. is the lad seated on the steps of the temple, a bit of pure *genre* that occurs again in Pinturicchio's fresco of 1501 at Spello, representing " Christ among the Doctors." Surely, however low Perugino may stand in our estimation, we should not dream of accusing him of suddenly, at the height of his fame, setting himself to imitate Pinturicchio, with the servility that is evident in the Caen " Sposalizio."

I have still another argument in support of my

[1] Perugia Gallery.

[Caen.

THE MARRIAGE OF THE VIRGIN

RAPHAEL

THE MARRIAGE OF THE VIRGIN

DRAWING OF A WOMAN

position. The woman in profile who closes in the composition to the right, is, with only imperceptible differences, so exactly identical with the drawing which is here reproduced,[1] that it is impossible to deny that one of these figures is a copy of the other. But which of the two is the original? It would be just possible for a person hard put to it to close his eyes and affirm that the "Sposalizio" was painted by Perugino, and that Pinturicchio, for his own amusement, afterwards copied one of the figures from the picture. But a serious examination shows that any such hypothesis is untenable. The drawing presents all the refined elegance, all the slightly ailing delicacy, which particularly characterize Pinturicchio, and which are quite as much his sign-mark as the technique and execution. From the point of view of quality, the difference in favour of the drawing is considerable. Not only does it possess a grace and distinction which the painting totally lacks, but the draperies are better treated, and the whole style is more vibrant. Compared with the drawing, the picture bears all the marks of a copy meticulously executed by a less skilful hand, capable of imitating rather than of creating. This being the case, and it being out of the question to suppose that Perugino lowered himself to a servile and disfiguring plagiarism from one of Pinturicchio's figures, we have a strong presumption in favour of doubting the attribution to Perugino of the altar-piece. This presumption changes to certainty when we look attentively, noting the differences of types, of character, and of colour, which the "Sposalizio" offers, when confronted with any indubitable work of Perugino.

[1] Uffizi, cornice 256, No. 364, black chalk heightened with white on light brown paper.

We are thus led to admit that the painter of the "Sposalizio," whoever he was, stands (in some respects) much nearer to Pinturicchio than he does to Perugino. His resemblances to the former are even more manifest in the types and the colour. The protrusion of the cheek-bone, the eyes showing a great deal of the white, the exaggerated brilliancy of the colouring, are never found in Perugino; while Pinturicchio from the Borgia Apartments up to the "Christ Bearing the Cross" in the Borromeo Gallery at Milan, invariably presents these characteristics.

If Perugino really were the author of the picture in question, our opinion of his artistic merit, low as it may be, would have to fall still lower; for he would prove himself in this work to be a servile imitator of Pinturicchio, his younger and incontestably inferior fellow-pupil. But what are we to think when we discover that the author of the "Sposalizio" imitated Raphael as well? I will not insist upon the resemblances which, in the general grouping of the figures, are manifest between the four people at the extreme left of the picture, and the four who are also at the left in Raphael's "Adoration of the Magi" in the Vatican. Neither will I insist on the hair of the High Priest, which stands out around his head as if electrified—a trait quite peculiar to Raphael. But the tiny and slightly mincing mouths, the flushed faces, the bony construction of the cheeks, and their rather puffy modelling, are all characteristics which separate us from Perugino to unite us to Raphael, who, in all these details, differs from his master. Finally, I may remark that the turbaned young woman, the third figure to the right, is a purely Raphaelesque type.

No! Perugino certainly did not imitate his

pupil : he did not steal from Pinturicchio. Perugino, despite his weaknesses as an artist, had the quality of being always himself, only changing through his own momentum, and not by impulsion from without. He could not, then, have been the author of the Caen "Sposalizio." Nor can a way of escape be found in the suggestion that perhaps he was responsible for the design, if not for the actual execution of the picture ; all the arguments that have been brought forward to show that he could not have painted the picture, prove, *à fortiori*, that he could not have designed it. Perugino was a total stranger to the "Sposalizio" at Caen. Who, then, was its author ? we must now ask ; and it is this question which I intend to try to answer.

II

As we have just seen, the author of the Caen "Sposalizio," in his choice of types, in his colour, and in his composition, shows a closer affinity with Pinturicchio than with Perugino. We have also observed that he bears trace to a notable degree of Raphael's influence. Of course it would be absurd to deny that Perugino's influence as well is felt in the picture. It appears clearly, for example, in the figure of the old man near St. Joseph, and in the fourth female to right. The painter whose name we are looking for must consequently have been formed by Pinturicchio, and influenced by Perugino and Raphael. In order that he should so very early have felt the impress of the latter, he must have been his fellow-pupil ; and, in fact, Raphael and he have this singular resemblance that, each in his own way,

they show in the same proportions, the double influence of Pinturicchio and of Perugino.

Now, of the companions of Raphael at Perugia,
two only have preserved the least shadow of reputation : Eusebio di San Giorgio, and Giovanni, called
Lo Spagna.   To one at all familiar with the works
of the latter painter,[1] his manner and his execution
will, before this, have been evident in the "Sposalizio" of Caen.

Let us begin with the types.   The Virgin has the
rounded oval, the large, unmodelled forehead, the
faintly-indicated eyebrows, the drooping eyes, the
rounded nostrils, and the pinched mouth, which
occur in Lo Spagna throughout his entire career.
We can see this type in one of his earliest works,
the altar-piece in the Perugia Gallery (Room XI.,
No. 7), and in a much later fresco, in the Municipio
at Spoleto, where it persists without change.   But
it is not necessary to go to Italy to find points of
comparison, when the Louvre offers us, in this
respect, almost all that we need.   Those who are
capable of changing a profile into a full face, and of
seeing the one in their mind, as clearly as they see
the other with their eyes, will not be long in perceiving the identity of the Virgin at Caen with the
Madonna of Lo Spagna in the Louvre (No. 1540),
or, better still, of the kneeling angels in the Vatican
"Nativity," of which the Louvre offers us a replica
(No. 1539).

The figure of St. Joseph is also that of the saint

---

[1] To those less familiar with this painter I recommend the
chapter relating to Lo Spagna in Cavalcaselle, the best chapter,
by the way, to make one understand the value of that truly
monumental work—a work which, of its kind, shows the same
energy, the same patient effort, that characterized so many Italians
of the heroic age, now so completely vanished.

THE ADORATION OF THE HOLY CHILD

in the Vatican "Nativity." We find there the same long nose, the same prominent cheek-bones, the same accentuated shadow in the hollow of the cheeks. He is, in fact, Lo Spagna's habitual type of old man; and we find him at least half a dozen times in that painter's masterpiece, "The Coronation of the Virgin," at Todi, dated 1511.

The woman in a hood, the third to the right, whose Raphaelesque look I have already mentioned, is of a type one might seek for in vain in Perugino; but she is often to be met with, on the other hand, in Lo Spagna, with more or less slight modification,—as, for example, in the "Coronation" already alluded to, where she is to be seen among the angels who are floating on the right, and also in the Assisi altarpiece, where she occupies the second place on the right. We find her again, isolated, in the "Beata Colomba da Rieti" in the Perugia Gallery (Room XI., No. 2). Two of the women have the sly look which is characteristic of Lo Spagna, and all have a yellowish tint. This is one of Lo Spagna's peculiarities, like the flushed cheeks of his men.[1]

We spoke in the beginning of the rather gaudy general effect of the colouring, and we have just glanced at the flesh tones. I must now note a few other peculiarities of colour habitual to Lo Spagna. The man at the extreme left, whom we have pointed out as very different in type and movement from the style of Perugino, differs still more from this painter in colour. His mantle is of a Chartreuse green which is never found in Perugino, but which is, on the contrary, very frequent in Lo Spagna. We find the exact shade, for example, in the garments of the floating angels in the Vatican "Nativity." The

[1] Notably in the "Coronation" of Todi and in the altar-piece of 1516 at S. Francesco in Assisi.

salmon pink of the scarves worn by the women in the "Sposalizio" is exactly the same tone as the draperies of the shepherds in the same picture. Finally, the grays and light blues which occur so often in the Caen altar-piece, are never found in exactly these shades in any truly authentic work by Perugino, while they are frequent in Lo Spagna's most carefully elaborated pictures.

It would not be suitable to take away from Perugino a work so universally known as the "Sposalizio" —a work, moreover, often cited as his masterpiece— if we had not superabundant proof. The reader, I trust, will therefore be patient with me if I insist on certain details whose triviality evidently escaped the special attention of the painter and which, for that reason—being executed by rote and, as it were, almost unconsciously—enable us to get a closer acquaintance with his habits. In the "Sposalizio" the ears have invariably the form which we see in Lo Spagna's "Madonna" in the Louvre; they are joined to the cheeks in a rather unusual way, and they are quite different from those of Perugino, both in general outline and in the shape of the cavity. The hands have so broad a palm that it almost amounts to a deformity, and that swollen second phalanx of the thumb that we can parallel not only in the "Madonna" of the Louvre, but everywhere in Lo Spagna. Perugino's hands are much finer and more delicate.

A detail even more typical is to be found in the way the draperies are disposed. It is instructive to compare, in this respect, the Caen "Sposalizio" with Lo Spagna's works on the one hand, and Perugino's on the other. The arrangement of draperies in the latter is more supple, more natural, more graceful; while in Lo Spagna's works they seem, to borrow

MADONNA AND CHILD

Cavalcaselle's expression, arranged by hand as on lay
figures.   The Virgin's torso is clothed in a sort of
shapeless sack, under which one can scarcely make
out her form.   St. Joseph also wears a garment that
looks like a sack, and the same might be said of
most of the figures in the picture.   As to the High
Priest's garment, I defy anyone to find the least indication of his body under that vague drapery, which
has the appearance of a decalcomania.   Let the
reader compare these draperies with those he can
see in Lo Spagna's better works—the " Madonna "
of the Louvre, the altar-piece at Assisi, the "Coronation " at Todi—and he will find the same peculiarities, the same weaknesses, the same meaningless
corkscrew writhings, the same incapacity to make us
realize the nude under the drapery.   In Lo Spagna,
the folds seldom have the angular decision that
Perugino gives them ;   they usually end up in a
round. Their characteristic, obvious to even a superficial examination, is a sort of corkscrew line, writhing
about, in a desperate effort to become functional.
We encounter this line everywhere in the Caen
" Sposalizio," notably under the Virgin's left hand,
and by the right hand of the woman who stands near
her, as well as on the right sleeve of St. Joseph.
Another sort of fold, extremely characteristic of Lo
Spagna's system, is the one formed by the mantles
at the place where, falling over the shoulder, they join
the arm.   They form there a concave fold, which is
continued by a convex curve opposite another fold,
exactly like itself.   Let the reader himself look for
this fold in the " Sposalizio," he will find it without
difficulty.

   We shall do well at this point to see what further
light is thrown upon the whole matter by the drawings
connected with this " Sposalizio."   Four only need

detain us. The well-known study in black chalk
in the Louvre for the Virgin's head (photo. Braun,
301) is so timid in handling, so poor in construction,
and of a type so different in essentials from Perugino, that years before it occurred to me to suspect
the authenticity of the Caen picture, I had ceased
believing this head to be his. Of exactly identical
character is the study for St. Joseph's profile in the
Musée Condé at Chantilly (photo. Braun, " Beaux
Arts," 99). In both drawings we note the same
meticulousness, the same timidity, the same system
of cross-hatching. But they have every aspect of
being not copies after the painting, but original
studies for it. The Joseph, moreover, bears all
over it the imprint of Lo Spagna's hand. A pen-
and-ink sketch at Brunswick for Joseph and the
five figures on his right, is even remoter from
Perugino than are the two heads. Not only is the
line inconceivably feeble, producing at times scarcely
the effect of free-hand drawing, but the hatching is
denser and minuter than it ever is in Perugino.
That here again we encounter Lo Spagna, we see
from such characteristic traits as the concave
thumbs, the straight line for Joseph's sleeve (cf. the
Uffizi cartoon for the Christ in the National Gallery
" Agony in the Garden"), and the extremely broad
face of the youth, which resembles one of the youths
in the Albertina drawing (Sc. Rom., 39). The
fourth of the sketches in question, is one in silver-
point heightened with white, in the Malcolm Collection at the British Museum (No. 156, photo. Braun,
" Beaux Arts," 98). Less, even, than in the others
can there be question here of Perugino's authorship.
It represents the three central figures, and is of such
a poverty as draughtsmanship, and so exaggeratedly
Lo Spagnesque, that I question whether it is not

LO SPAGNA

SKETCH FOR FIGURES IN THE CAEN "SPOSALIZIO"

perhaps a copy after the picture by Lo Spagna's well-known assistant and follower, Jacopo Siculo. At all events, not one of these four drawings corroborates the attribution of the picture to Perugino.

III

We have now adduced proof to demonstrate that the "Sposalizio" of Caen, inasmuch as it shows greater affinities with Pinturicchio and Raphael than with Perugino, cannot have been executed, or even designed, by the latter. We have also pointed out that the distinctive characteristics of this work are in perfect agreement with the manner of Lo Spagna. In speaking of his altar-piece at Perugia, Cavalcaselle says that it shows a very judicious combination of elements borrowed from Raphael, from Perugino, and from Pinturicchio. We who have made, on our side, an analysis of the "Sposalizio," know to what degree its author shows precisely these aptitudes for assimilating impressions, and we do not hesitate to pronounce that the details of this composition bear the unquestionable marks of Lo Spagna.

The author of the "Sposalizio" of Caen was therefore this Spagna who, in his earliest pictures, constantly imitated Raphael. When he began, he was hardly twenty years of age, but his subjection to Raphael only went on increasing with his years, as all his subsequent works show. He is the same painter who was so feeble in invention that, in his most important compositions, he remained either a mere copyist (as in his Todi "Coronation," which he borrowed from Ghirlandaio), or a compiler, as in the greater part of his works. Towards Raphael, in particular, his attitude was so humble, that we still possess from his hand an exact copy[1] of the Bergamo " St. Sebastian," a picture of the master's Peruginesque period.

All this being so, one cannot help asking this question : is it possible that a man so destitute of creative power, an artist so feeble that he could not walk without, as it were, leaning upon someone else, a painter who only lived on the alms of Pinturicchio and Perugino and Raphael,—is it possible that such a man should have suddenly conceived a composition so happy that Raphael, the artist to whom he owed most, should have instantly desired to copy it ? The answer we may be able to give to this question, will confirm or weaken the third proposition I enounced at the beginning, namely, that Raphael, for his " Sposalizio," did not draw his inspiration from the Caen altar-piece, but that, on the contrary, it was the Caen picture that was borrowed outright from Raphael.

Granting that Lo Spagna not only painted but also designed the " Sposalizio," the answer to the question, given the immense difference of genius between Lo Spagna and Raphael, is obvious. The sun does not borrow his light from the moon. Raphael certainly would not have dreamt of imitating his humble reflector, Lo Spagna. However, let us be patient awhile, and find new proofs to convince those who may still remain unconvinced.

The question would be of course settled if we knew the exact date at which the Caen "Sposalizio" was executed. As we all know, this painting, up to

---

[1] This picture belongs to Mr. Denman Ross, of Cambridge, U.S.A. Reproduced in "Les Peintures Italiennes de New York et Boston" ("Gazette des Beaux Arts," Troisième Période, tome xv., p. 212).

THE CORONATION OF THE VIRGIN

the end of the last century, occupied the altar of the chapel of St. Joseph, in the Cathedral of Perugia. Although it was ordered in 1495, it was not yet begun in November, 1500 : that is the only documentary evidence that has so far come to hand about the date of its execution.[1] To determine its date we must compare it to Lo Spagna's dated works. The first which we know of is the "Coronation" at Todi, of 1511, which we have already had occasion to mention. In this picture—his masterpiece—Lo Spagna seems barely to have attained his full maturity. He is still penetrated with a youthful freshness, but, at the same time, the different elements of which his style is composed, are better assimilated than in the Perugia altar-piece, or in the "Sposalizio," or in the "Nativity" of the Vatican. On the other hand, his characteristic traits—the exaggerated relief of the cheek-bones, the ambiguous glance, the yellowish flesh, the heavy draperies— are all more clearly accentuated. These three works, where his peculiar mannerisms are less felt than in the Todi "Coronation," must, on that account, precede it in date. But between these three pictures themselves there are notable differences : the altar-piece at Perugia is the one which least suggests the period of his maturity ; the one which is nearest to it is the Vatican "Nativity." We can thus place the date of the latter fairly near to that of the "Coronation," with which it has many points of resemblance, that is to say, somewhere about 1511. I do not think I go too far in stating that it could not have been earlier than 1508. If we could get an approximate date for the

---

[1] The name of Perugino, we may remark, is not mentioned in any of the documents which speak of the "Sposalizio." Vasari was the first to attribute it to him.

Perugia altar-piece, we should be close to the date of the "Sposalizio," whose style places it just between these two.   Signor Cavalcaselle says about this altar-piece, that it shows Lo Spagna's skill in combining to his advantage what he took from Raphael, Perugino, Pinturicchio : when he speaks of the Virgin, he describes her as "full of a Raphaelesque freshness."   Later, he says, "There is nothing more noteworthy than this application of the use of oils, that we find in Raphael after he made the acquaintance of the Florentines ; the clear tints are laid on upon the white ground.   But this is not the only side on which the altar-piece of Perugia *approaches closely to the 'Sposalizio' of Raphael*. The resemblance appears clearly in all the forms, as well as in the dryness, in the sense of effort, and in the stiffness of the execution of the members." Signor Cavalcaselle was more than right.   It is impossible that Lo Spagna could have painted his altar-piece earlier than Raphael his "Sposalizio," when he so clearly imitates this work.   The approximate date of the Perugia picture is therefore *at the earliest* 1504, the year in which Raphael painted his "Sposalizio."

But the "Sposalizio" of Caen has more points in common with the Vatican "Nativity," than with the Perugia altar-piece, and it indicates a more advanced maturity in the artist's talent.   It follows, therefore— the approximate dates for the two pictures being, for the one 1504, and for the other 1508—that the "Sposalizio" should be placed between these two dates, nearer to the latter than to the former; it could not, then, have been painted before 1506, two years or so after the famous picture of Raphael.

IV

I have been trying, by means of technical considerations, to establish the author of the Caen
"Sposalizio" as Lo Spagna instead of Perugino,
and to prove that this picture, far from being
the model which inspired Raphael, was, on the contrary, only an imitation of Raphael's masterpiece.
I trust I may not weary the reader too much by
discussing a few more points regarding these two
compositions, and the differences we can note in
them.   A very curious fact is that the "Sposalizio," the Marriage of the Virgin, a subject that
is frequently to be met with in Italian painting,
has been very seldom treated as a tall composition.
The most famous representations of this subject—
Giotto's at Padua, Lorenzo's at Viterbo, Ghirlandaio's at S. Maria Novella—are much wider
than they are high.   Perugino himself made no
exception to this rule.   His "Sposalizio" at
Fano, dated 1497, follows the established models;
it is almost identical with another "Sposalizio"
in the monastery of San Girolamo, near Spello,
painted fifteen years or so earlier, not by Perugino,
but by some one of his nameless fellow-pupils.   The
identity of these two compositions, despite the
fifteen years which separate them, shows that the
habit of treating this subject *in breadth* was so deep-
rooted, that it would not have occurred either to
Perugino or to any painter of the Umbrian school,
to break with the tradition.   And those who have
studied the history of composition know well what
supreme genius it requires to introduce any radical
change in this branch of art.

It may be, of course, pure coincidence, but the

only other "Sposalizio" which, to my knowledge, is higher than it is broad, is that of Lorenzo Costa in the gallery of Bologna.

Another curious circumstance is that, in most of the pictures representing this subject, Joseph is placed on the spectator's left and the Virgin on the right. This arrangement of the figures is an invariable peculiarity of all works of pure Umbrian character. Raphael took the contrary course, placing Joseph to the right and the Virgin to the left; an innovation which, we may be sure, was not due to pure caprice, nor to a sheer desire to upset tradition. There, once again, we find a singular identity of arrangement between Raphael and Costa.

There is another point in which Raphael's "Sposalizio" differs from the other versions, and especially from those of the Umbrian school. In those, the budding rod which Joseph holds is stiff and upright; in Raphael's picture, the rod which Joseph holds delicately between his thumb and forefinger, rests upon his shoulder. Here again we have a stranger and stranger coincidence, down to the slightest details, between Raphael and Costa.

Each one of these coincidences, considered separately, might be set down to chance, but we find three together. Here is another: in both pictures, one of St. Joseph's feet is straight while the other is bent, against all common sense, in a way to make a right angle with the first. Perhaps this is only chance,[1] but perhaps it is something else.

---

[1] We know that Costa painted his "Sposalizio" in 1505, a year after that of Raphael. Whoever has had any experience in morphological studies as applied to the Italian schools of painting, could not, even for a moment, hold the idea that Costa's inflexible character would have permitted him to borrow no matter what,

Raphael, as we know him in his earlier years, was by no means an adventurous spirit, eager to break with tradition. On the contrary, he loved to walk in the beaten paths. Nevertheless, a close examination of his youthful works reveals many divergences from the Umbrian school, divergences which, given his happy docility, it is not easy to account for. One may therefore hazard an hypothesis, which is not based on documents, but which, in its humble way, like the hypotheses of Copernicus and Newton, rests only on observation, and has no other proof than that it explains a group of facts otherwise inexplicable. This hypothesis is that the many differences one observes between Perugino and the divine Raphael, his docile pupil, came from an earlier training to which the latter had been subjected, from habits formed before he came to Perugino, which he was never able quite to forget. This hypothesis would lead us to consider all the works of Raphael belonging to his Peruginesque period, as a compromise between two opposed sets of tradition : the later, that of Perugino, more obvious, more on the surface ; the earlier having left more traces in Raphael upon the fundamental elements of his style, upon what one might call the grammar of the art of construction.

The hypothesis once admitted, Raphael's first master would turn out to have been one of his compatriots of Urbino, Timoteo Viti, himself a pupil of Francia and Costa, and a continuer of their tradition. A sagacious observer will remark that, in his earliest works, Raphael's characteristic traits do not in any way recall Perugino, but ally themselves with the school of Ferrara-Bologna. One might see

from a work painted so far away and done by an artist twenty-three years younger than himself.

nothing but pure accident there; but I dare affirm that no mathematician expert in the calculation of probabilities would venture to attribute to chance so large a group of coincidences. We have, therefore, every right to accept a theory which throws light upon so many otherwise obscure points :   Timoteo Viti, a painter of the school of Ferrara-Bologna, who was living at Urbino when Raphael was a child, undoubtedly gave him his first lessons, and transmitted to him the traditions he had himself received from Costa and Francia.[1]

Admitting this, all the strange coincidences which we have noted between the Raphael " Sposalizio " and Costa's are explained by their having common traditions; and if the docile Raphael painted a "Sposalizio" different from Perugino's, the explanation is not the improbable one that he was suddenly seized with a spirit of independence and the desire to be original, but the simple, probable one that another model was haunting his mind to such a degree as to make the resulting composition a compromise between the traditions of the school of Ferrara-Bologna and that of Perugia.

This long digression is designed to lead only to this conclusion : it is more than likely that the "Sposalizio" of Raphael, in its essential composition, was inspired by the Ferrara-Bologna school. This would certainly prove that the composition was his own, and was not taken direct from his Umbrian master, Perugino.

Raphael profited by Perugino's teaching in only one thing. The painter of Urbino, the artist who, among all the artists of the world, has attained the most marvellous effects of space, owed the revelation of this quality, which is his supreme quality, to

[1] I need scarcely add that this theory was Morelli's.

Perugino, who before him was the most successful
master of space composition. I doubt if a painter
brought up entirely in the school of Ferrara-Bologna
could have composed an effect of space such as we
find in Raphael's "Sposalizio," which gives one so
penetrating a sense of well-being that, gazing on it, we
have a pleasure such as pure spirits disencumbered of
their bodies might feel. What breadth there is in his
middle distances, pure and cool, filled with an air so
soft and fresh ! What repose in the delicate vapours
at the horizon ! How uplifting and how soothing
the colonnades of his temple !

Now Perugino, although he is inferior to Raphael,
is less so in his effects of space than elsewhere. If
he had painted the " Sposalizio " of Caen, which represents a scene in the open air, he would have given
us a space composition not so inferior to Raphael's.
And one of the strongest reasons we have for ex-
culpating Perugino from the charge of having painted
the Caen altar-piece, is that this picture is totally
lacking in the quality in which Perugino especially
excelled. What has happened, in this " Sposalizio,"
to the middle distances ? where is this dream-like
colonnade ? where is the horizon which fades away
like music dying in the distance ? Lo Spagna, who
of all the Umbrians was least gifted with a feeling
of space, did not appreciate these qualities in his
model, and therefore could not render them.

He must have seen Raphael's " Sposalizio," and
have retained a recollection of it sufficiently precise
to repeat its general disposition when he came to
make his own composition ; but, being exclusively
Umbrian, his spirit could not retain anything that
went contrary to his Umbrian tradition and habits.
In his " Sposalizio," as in all similar pictures of his
school, the Virgin is at the right and Joseph at the

left; he broadened Raphael's composition, and spoiled the marvellous distribution of the groups which Raphael had made; he brought the temple near and made it vulgar.   In a word, he took one of the loveliest compositions in existence, to reduce it to the measure of his insipid and provincial talent.

ALESSIO BALDOVINETTI AND THE NEW "MADONNA" OF THE LOUVRE

A NUMBER of years ago, turning over one day the photograph albums in the hospitable shop of MM. Braun, Clément et Cie, my eye fell by chance upon the reproduction of a "Madonna" attributed to Piero dei Franceschi. I recognized at once the style of a master much rarer, quite as interesting, and sometimes almost as great as Piero,—the Florentine Alessio Baldovinetti. This "Madonna" I knew had once been in the Duchâtel collection ; but I tried in vain to find out what had become of it since. I had the good fortune to meet it at last in the collection of the Duc de la Trémoïlle. The picture far sur- passed my expectations. The Madonna, seated on a throne which dominated a landscape of noble out- lines, was at once delicate and winning, as well as possessed of an almost hieratic majesty. Dirt, bad varnish, repaint, had done their worst to spoil her beauty, but they did not succeed in taking away the pleasure she gave. The original grandeur and nobility of the conception shone through them as through a light veil.

When I went away, I asked myself rather sadly if I should ever have the pleasure of seeing her again, and where. The unhappy wanderings of pictures are never ended until they find their last asylum in one of the public collections of Europe. Then we can have at least the satisfaction of knowing them definitely installed in a permanent home; and yet such collections seem to put every conceivable obstacle in the way of our enjoyment. Pictures are classified on almost any principle except the æsthetic, the only legitimate one in matters of art; a masterpiece runs every risk of being stuck, like a postage-stamp, on a wall covered with paintings that have nothing but historic or archæological interest to recommend them, instead of being, as they should be, isolated in a special niche like the image of a jealous god. Nevertheless, in spite of these drawbacks, one rarely sees a real work of art in a private collection without hoping for a speedy end to its migrations. I heard with joy, therefore, that this lovely " Madonna " had entered the gallery of the Louvre. It is assuredly the most important Italian picture which for several years past has come into any of the public collections of Europe.

I shall not attempt here to describe the beauty of this " Madonna." As far as its charm can be evoked by words, it has been done by M. Ary Renan, in his excellent article in the "Chronique des Arts" (March 5th, 1898), and the faithful reproduction here given, only serves to illustrate his discriminating and eloquent appreciation. My task is the more humble one of trying to prove that the Louvre's new treasure is not the work of Piero della Francesca, to whom it was attributed when it was sold, but of Alessio Baldovinetti. Even on this point M. Renan has so far anticipated not only my attribution, but my arguments, that little remains for me to add; I can only go more carefully into detail than he has done. I should add also that M. Renan is not the only one who deprives my attribution of all claims to originality; in looking through what has been written by other critics upon Baldovinetti, and

PIERO DELLA FRANCESCA

[*Sta. Maria delle Grazie, Sinigaglia.*

THE MADONNA AND CHILD

particularly what has been said by the most authoritative of all, the lamented Signor Cavalcaselle, I ascertained that he had already, many years ago, given this " Madonna " to Alessio.

I

The scarcity of his works, not his lack of talent, and also, it must be added, the surprising inequality of his achievements, account for the fact that, except among specialists, Alessio Baldovinetti is hardly more than a name—if so much. A few words about him will, therefore, not be inappropriate. He was born in 1427 and died in 1499. History does not tell us who was the first master to put a brush into his hand; but to know who was literally the first instructor of a painter is a question of slight importance. It is of much greater consequence to find out what spirit influenced an artist in his youth, who moulded and developed his talent and determined his artistic style. In this, the really vital matter, historians with their documents seldom give us any help. It is a matter which we must establish for ourselves by the study of the artist's own works, and by determining their relation to those of his predecessors.

First of all, then, our task is to examine Alessio Baldovinetti's works and, to begin with, those of his paintings whose authenticity has never been called in question. The earliest of these is the splendid fresco which he executed in 1462 for the cloister at the entrance to the SS. Annunziata at Florence, a fresco of remarkable beauty in spite of its present ruined state—the parts done *al secco* having long since disappeared, taking with them all the charm of colour

that the faces could ever have had. Here is revealed an artist who, though he is undoubtedly
sensitive to beauty of type and grace of movement,
concentrates his most earnest attention upon a naturalistic rendering of detail and landscape. "He
loved to paint landscapes," says Vasari, "and he
drew them after nature, exactly as they are. That
is why you can see in his pictures, rivers, bridges,
rocks, grass and fruit trees, roads, fields, towns,
castles, stretches of sand, and an infinite number of
other things." Messer Giorgio no doubt had this
fresco in mind while writing these lines, and they fit
closely. But he forgot to mention what I find especially worthy of admiration, the art which could
group in one harmonious composition these innumer-
able details, and—what is even more surprising—
could give such an impression of height, of distance
to the landscape and sky which rise and spread
around the figures. We should search in vain among
earlier pictures for effects of space comparable to
this; and, even among those who, in later times,
have been the greatest masters of space-composition
—Perugino, Raphael, Poussin, Claude Lorrain and
Turner—very few have equalled, and almost none
have surpassed this achievement of Baldovinetti.

In 1463 Alessio composed a cartoon for a Nativity,
which was faithfully copied in *intarsia* by Giuliano da
Maiano, for the Sacristy of the Florence Cathedral,
where it is still to be seen. The composition closely
resembles that of the preceding fresco.

In 1467 our artist decorated *al fresco* the interior
of a Holy Sepulchre in the Chapel of the Rucellai
family; the painting represents Christ rising from
the tomb, between two adoring angels. This important work still exists, and merits more attention
than it has received. Signor Cavalcaselle does not

[*Uffizi, Florence.*

THE MADONNA AND CHILD

DETAIL OF AN ALTAR-PIECE

THE MADONNA AND CHILD

speak of it in his monumental work; nor is it mentioned by recent writers, so far as I am aware. The colour is well preserved, and is of a splendour which we are not accustomed to associate with Florentine art, for the brocades rival the gorgeousness of Crivelli's or Matteo di Giovanni's. But the types are inferior; one would say that the painter took no interest in anything except the garments.

The lack of regard for beauty, joined to a too great preoccupation with the problems of execution, technique and science, appears still more clearly in an altar-piece from S. Trinità, now in the Florence Academy, which was finished in February, 1472. This picture represents the "Trinity," with cherubs and kneeling saints. The parts where the colour has not peeled off have almost the depth of enamel: the drawing has great, almost too great, precision; but the modelling and the movement of the figures are excellent. Much as one may admire the detail, as a whole it is unsatisfactory; the artist had given place to the craftsman.

Baldovinetti made every conceivable experiment with colour and medium; he rediscovered mosaic; he occupied himself with everything, except with painting for art's sake. For him, as for the other Florentine naturalists, painting was interesting only in so far as it offered scientific problems for solution. The few remaining fragments of the frescoes, executed by Alessio in his last years at S. Trinità, show no change in his intentions or his manner. Throughout his entire career he was faithful to the same style, to the same types, losing his original refinement and grace, in the measure that he became more and more absorbed in his craft.

These, then, are the works of Baldovinetti which have never been called in question, and whose actual dates one knows. There are two other paintings which he must have executed between 1460 and 1465 : the earliest and at the same time most beautiful of them is the admirable " Madonna " recently sold by Baldovinetti's descendants to Mme. Edouard André of Paris. It is a picture that has neither the grandeur nor the delicacy of the one just bought by the Louvre; but its fortunate state of preservation enables one to do justice to the exquisite delicacy of the drawing, and to the subtle modelling of the cloudlets in the pearly sky. The same type of Virgin, with features somewhat pinched, is found in the second of these works, the interesting altar-piece in the Uffizi : it is a work of delicate sentiment and subtle craftsmanship.

Vasari is responsible for an error current about two other of Alessio Baldovinetti's paintings. In the Portuguese chapel at San Miniato, finished in 1466, there are frescoes representing the " Four Evangelists " and the " Four Fathers of the Church," as well as a panel with the " Annunciation " : above one sees, again in fresco, a garden with trees. All these, ascribed by Vasari to Pietro Pollaiuolo, are given by Albertini in his " Memoriale," published fifty years earlier, to Alessio Baldovinetti. He was right and Vasari wrong : this is perfectly clear after a moment's examination. In fact, there is not to-day a single competent critic who hesitates to ascribe them all to Alessio. The frescoes have suffered greatly from the peeling off of the colours ; but the " Annunciation " is well preserved and of great beauty. The space which it had to fill required a long, narrow panel, a form which was afterwards adopted by Verrocchio [1] and Leonardo. [2] Here again we observe a refined and solemn sentiment joined

[1] Uffizi, No. 1288.   [2] Louvre, No. 1265.

[Mme. André, Paris.

THE MADONNA AND CHILD

to great precision and extreme delicacy of workman-
ship.

Another " Annunciation," formerly in San Giorgio,
and attributed by Vasari to Pesellino, is now in the
Uffizi (No. 56). As Baldovinetti's manner is even
more clearly visible in it than in the paintings at
San Miniato, all the critics of importance [1] agree in
recognizing it as his. It is a work of considerable
beauty and charm, tranquil, fresh and delicate. The
most striking part is the angel with yellow curls,
who rushes forward, his arms reverently crossed, im-
patient to deliver his message. This work seems
to me still to belong to Baldovinetti's earlier years,
when as yet he was more artist than man of science.
We have now come to the end of the list of pictures
generally accepted as Alessio's. There is, however,
one more, beside the new acquisition of the Louvre :
it is in the Florence Academy (No. 33), and attributed
there to Fra Angelico.[2] Many years ago I had
already observed a very close connection between
this panel—which contains the " Marriage of Cana,"
the " Baptism," and the " Transfiguration "—and
the works of Baldovinetti. But I doubted his
capacity for so much freshness and grace, and was
inclined to see in them the youthful hand of some
gifted disciple, until my friend, Mr. Herbert Horne,
told me that this panel could not date from a time
later than 1448.[3] Then I understood clearly why
these little pictures had such an unwonted charm.

[1] Notably Cavalcaselle and Dr. Bode.
[2] Photographed by Anderson, Nos. 6553 to 6555.
[3] Mr. Horne draws his conclusion from the manuscript
chronicle of Benedetto Dei, at the Magliabecchiani Library at
Florence. I do not wish to enter here into further details on
this point, for I trust Mr. Horne will soon find occasion to speak
at length of it, and also of many other interesting questions relating to the study of Florentine art.

It is due to the fact that their painter was not then twenty years old, for in 1447 no one certainly but Alessio could have painted in this style.

All the differences in type and form which distinguish them from Alessio's other works—and these differences are, in fact, extremely slight—are explained when we learn that a period of fifteen years elapsed between this panel and the first of his hitherto recognized works. It has a double interest, therefore ; on the one hand it shows us Alessio's beginnings, and enables us, as no other work, to follow the development of his spirit and his style, which, without it, would remain quite obscure ; and on the other hand it brings us near to the artist who was the first to form our painter, and helps us to determine his identity.

These earliest works of Alessio, then, bear witness to a mastery of movement and form which he never surpassed ; furthermore, they have a charm of expression, a grace, a vivacity and a daintiness of colouring, which one finds less and less as his work progresses. In going over the whole career of the artist, from the small pictures where still lingers a little of the spirit of Fra Angelico, to the hardened naturalism of the fragments at Santa Trinità, one sees clearly that Alessio possessed in his youth the genuine artist's temperament ; then, as his mind developed and attained its full power, it turned out not only that he was more of a craftsman than an artist, but enough of the mere craftsman to kill the artist. In the course of this evolution we might well expect a moment when the artist's temperament and the craftsman's spirit should find themselves in exact equilibrium, and should act in perfect harmony. At such a moment Alessio Baldovinetti would have been able to produce a masterpiece superior in scope

[*Private Collection, Florence.*

THE MADONNA AND CHILD

[*Uffizi, Florence.*

THE MADONNA AND CHILD
DETAIL OF AN ALTAR-PIECE

to his first naïve pictures, and in beauty to his last naturalistic experiments. We shall see that this was exactly what did happen.

II

Students who are acquainted with the too rare works of Domenico Veneziano and who are able to bring them clearly to mind, cannot fail, at the sight of these first efforts of Alessio, to note a marked resemblance between them. This is not confined to types alone (as the bride in the " Marriage of Cana," who resembles St. Lucy in Domenico's Uffizi altarpiece) ; it is not only a likeness in the gay blond colouring, but it is an undoubted analogy in what is more essential still, in form and action. In Baldovinetti's picture, the gesture of the page who is pouring out water is copied almost line for line from that of the executioner in Domenico's " Martyrdom of St. Lucy." [1] But here we are not concerned with a simple plagiarism : the resemblance does not come from a servile imitation, but from the fact that Alessio had been taught by Domenico to give this gesture to all figures of analogous movement. It proves that Domenico was really Baldovinetti's master ; and a curious fact confirms the theory : the hands of the people in Veneziano's pictures are usually drawn with bent fingers, half covered by the thumb and index, and this same precise mannerism is found in Baldovinetti's earliest paintings. A good instance is the left hand of the man opposite Christ, at the end of the table, in the " Marriage of Cana." In Alessio's later works this peculiarity disappears—a fact which proves that when Alessio painted this panel the in-

[1] Berlin, No. 64 ; photographed by Hanfstaengl, No. 670.

fluence of Domenico upon him was still recent and strong. The force of this influence betrays itself elsewhere, up to the end of Alessio's career, in one trait and another. In all his " Madonnas " that we know, he follows Domenico's type with a fidelity even greater than that of any of this master's accredited pupils. It would be hard to find a resemblance so close between any work of Piero dei Franceschi's and his master Domenico Veneziano, as we may descry between a " Madonna" by Alessio belonging to the present writer, and Domenico's " Madonna " in the Uffizi.[1]

In the two " Nativities," and in the altar-piece of the Uffizi, Alessio's Virgins wear exactly the same head-dress as does the " Madonna " of Domenico in the Uffizi ; and Mme. André's " Madonna " wears a kerchief which recalls that of Veneziano's " Madonna" in the National Gallery. In this latter fresco there is also a God the Father whose type we find again in Baldovinetti's " Trinity." From Domenico Veneziano, again, Alessio must have taken his practice of encrusting his thrones with porphyry, and placing them in flower-gardens.

There is no *à priori* difficulty to prevent our assuming that these two painters did actually stand in the relation of master and pupil, for Domenico was decorating the choir of Sant' Egidio at Florence between the years 1439 and 1445, just when Alessio, at the age of from twelve to eighteen, was most likely to be set, as was the usual fifteenth-century

[1] This " Madonna," until it came into the author's possession, passed for Piero dei Franceschi's. I shall not attempt here to substantiate my conviction that it is Baldovinetti's, nor, perchance, will it be necessary, if I succeed in persuading the reader that the Louvre picture is by him. Yet the resemblance to Veneziano is so great that more than one critic has seriously held it to be his.

ALESSIO BALDOVINETTI

THE NATIVITY

Florentine practice, to learn how to paint. Furthermore, we know that the series of these frescoes upon
which Castagno and Domenico Veneziano worked,
was, as a matter of fact, completed by Baldovinetti.
It is true that this did not take place until 1460, but
I believe Baldovinetti would not have been chosen
for this task, if it had not been felt that his style
would readily harmonize with the paintings already
existing. And just here I may add that, after
having left Domenico Veneziano, Alessio must have
felt the influence of Paolo Uccello, and, still more, of
Castagno. In fact, we know from his memoirs (for
Baldovinetti left memoirs) that he worked with
Castagno in 1454.

But I must not stray from the point I have to
make, which is to prove that Alessio was formed
chiefly by Domenico Veneziano. This master had,
it is universally admitted, another disciple far more
famous than our artist, Piero dei Franceschi. The
difference in character between Piero and Alessio is
as great as that which, to take an instance from
Greek literature, divides Pindar from Bacchilydes :
these two poets, nevertheless, made use of the same
grammar, the same style : at times the resemblance
between them is so striking, that not a few of the
strophes of the one might easily be attributed to the
other, if there were any uncertainty. But, in reality,
there is, between the talents of the two painters,
less distance than between the two poets. The
best productions of Alessio are rather different from
than inferior to those of Piero dei Franceschi. His
lesser reputation is due much more to the rarity and
inequality of his works than to the inferiority of his
gifts. It must be admitted, however, that he does
not deserve so high a rank, but that is because
he fails to maintain the high level of art held by

Piero and all other masters of the first order, not because he never attained it.

In the new Louvre "Madonna" we have Alessio at his best. She belongs to the happy moment of perfect balance between his artistic temperament and his scientific spirit, that moment of which I have spoken just now as propitious to the creation of something remarkable. That Alessio's masterpiece should be ascribed, as it is, to his fellow-pupil, Piero dei Franceschi, is by no means surprising, if we consider how faithfully both painters preserved their master's tradition, and if we add that in this "Madonna" the difference of *quality* between their talents is reduced to a minimum. It remains, notwithstanding, and may be recognized not only in the general conception, but in all sorts of little details as well.

The difference I shall now try to point out, and thus, I hope, prove conclusively that Alessio, and not Piero dei Franceschi, was the painter of this picture. Piero is happily too well known to require any fresh words of characterization here.[1] Compared with Baldovinetti, he is sterner and harder and more monumental. The word "delicate" could never be employed in speaking of him; neither could one call his work "refined"—not that it lacks refinement, but it belongs, so to speak, to an entirely different sphere. Well! the Madonna of the Duchâtel collection is majestic, hieratically majestic, but she is very refined, very delicate : she is neither massive nor monumental. Piero's Madonnas have a fixed and severe physiognomy, massive structure and immobile pose. In vain would one look among his pictures for a single personage who betrays a

---

[1] I have touched upon Piero in my book upon the "Central Italian Painters of the Renaissance," pp. 68-75.

[Uffizi, Florence.

THE ANNUNCIATION

fleeting emotion. The expression of his almost always imposing figures is the expression of the entire character, or, at most, of the whole action represented. Never a smile, never a touch of tenderness. How different from all this is the Madonna who forms the subject of our present discussion, with her refined features and her pensive gaze of adoration—a look that unveils her inner life, a look that will soon develop into the mystery which we feel in the face of the Mona Lisa! How different is Piero, even when he approaches this type of woman, as in his Madonna in the "Nativity" in the National Gallery! On the other hand, Piero constructs his figures far better. The modelling of his torsos is decided and powerful, while that of Alessio —this Madonna is an instance—is scarcely passable. Note the difference between the torso of our Louvre Madonna and the torso of the Virgin in Piero's Madonna at Sinigaglia.

Another striking difference between the new acquisition of the Louvre and all the works of Piero is the landscape. Piero seems never to have felt the poetry of space in the way we find it here, or, still more, in the Annunziata fresco at Florence. Piero's landscape is not really more rich in detail, but it seems so, because it lacks unity, because the forms are smaller, and because it is not in perfect harmony with the figures. His landscapes, such as those of the "Nativity," or the Uffizi "Portraits of the Duke and Duchess of Urbino," are delightful, it is true, but they lack the poetical and suggestive charm which made of Baldovinetti's landscapes the model not only for Pollaiuolo and Verrocchio, but even for Leonardo.

Coming down to minor details, let us begin with examining the features of the Madonna. The eyes are not so protruding as Piero's, the nose is more delicate and aquiline, the mouth is smaller, the lips are thinner. All these traits you will find almost invariably in no matter which one of Alessio's pictures, above all in Mme André's " Madonna." The hands are similar to the hands in that picture, and to those of the Virgin in the Uffizi, and, allowing for the difference of gesture, to every hand that Baldovinetti ever drew. The hands of Piero dei Franceschi, even when the gesture is identical, have a totally different form, are less flat, more massive in bone and flesh ; his wrists are also more powerful, as one can see by a single glance at the hands of the Virgins in the London " Nativity " and the Brera altar-piece. The Madonna's kerchief is not found in any work by Piero, while its resemblance with the kerchief of Mme. André's " Madonna," and that of the Virgin in the San Miniato " Annunciation " is most striking. The same may be said of the folds of drapery which, in Piero, are more angular and more complicated, while here they undulate or form large creases, as we find them in Alessio, especially in his early pictures.[1]

The Child is not yet that doll endowed with the absurd sagacity of a patriarch which we see later in Alessio, sometimes as a cherub, sometimes as an angel, and sometimes as the Infant Christ. He is not so fat as these, but his head is already too large, out of all proportion with his body, and his cheek is swollen in a way most characteristic of Baldovinetti's brush. He bears a certain resemblance to the Christ Child of Domenico Veneziano in the National Gallery fresco ; but he has absolutely nothing in common with the stolid young Hercules, who

[1] Particularly in the "Baptism" and the "Transfiguration" of the Florence Academy.

ALESSIO BALDOVINETTI

THE MARRIAGE OF CANA.

[*Accademia, Florence.*

DOMENICO VENEZIANO

[*Berlin.*]

THE MARTYRDOM OF ST. LUCY (?)

appears in all the works executed by Piero himself, or coming from his atelier.[1]

The Madonna's seat has the classic form which, under different aspects, one frequently meets with in *quattrocento* pictures ; but, at least to my knowledge, the exact shape of this chair, with the rose carved on the arm, is only to be found once again : it is the throne of the Madonna in Baldovinetti's altar-piece in the Uffizi.

Let us now turn to the landscape. I have already tried to describe its general character ; and we have seen that it offers no particular points of resemblance with Piero's backgrounds. It remains for us to seek for similarities of detail which may exist between this and other landscapes of Alessio's. A photograph of the fresco at the Annunziata would suffice, without further inquiry, to convince the reader of general and particular likenesses. The description I took from Vasari, a description which so perfectly fits the one, applies equally well to the other : the same vast cliff which rises obliquely towards the sky, the same pools, the same winding streams, which flow beneath the same arched bridges. The resemblance in details is scarcely less striking if we take the landscape in Mme. André's picture.

It is useless to go further. It would be hard to find a closer analogy in conception, forms, details, than what we have discovered between this panel and the works of Baldovinetti. As he was Piero's fellow-pupil, their pictures have a decided family resemblance, and it is not at all surprising that an unsigned work by the less known of these two painters should have been attributed to the more famous. But, as we have seen, if we put aside the

---

[1] Cf. the Brera altar-piece, another in the Perugia Gallery, and the " Madonna " at S. Maria delle Grazie at Sinigaglia.

general resemblance, which can do no more than furnish an indication as to the school a work of art belongs to, not as to its precise author, we find that this " Madonna " betrays none of the characteristics of Piero, while it possesses all those of Baldovinetti. Baldovinetti, therefore, was its author; and he painted it just at that period of his maturity when he had not yet forsaken the flowery meads of art for the stony paths of science. Alessio could scarcely have executed this masterpiece after 1460. The excellence of the picture helps us to understand better the great influence he seems to have exercised upon his contemporaries in Florence ; for he was not only the master of Cosimo Roselli and of Ghirlandaio, but also of two men of genius, Verrocchio and Antonio Pollaiuolo—and through them Alessio stands for more than a little in the making of Leonardo.

THE BRITISH MUSEUM "RAPHAEL"
CARTOON

A FEW years ago the British Museum acquired a Cartoon in black chalk, attributed to Raphael, which bore marks indicating that it had been used for transfer to panel or canvas. It contains the Virgin seated, and holding the Child, who half stands, half kneels, leaning his little head against his mother's neck, and stretching his right arm over her left breast. The composition is exquisite, with great dignity of style and a penetrating charm. The sentiment is undeniably Raphaelesque, and both the types and the poses recall that great master. It is a free translation of Raphael's "Vierge avec l'Enfant debout," and it is rather curious that no contemporary critic (of the old school, I mean) has jumped to the conclusion that this drawing was the actual one Raphael made use of for the picture. However that may be, I have not heard of anyone attributing it to Raphael, at least since its acquisition by the British Museum drew a certain amount of attention to it. Almost unanimous opinion has assigned it to one of the followers of Fra Bartolommeo and Andrea del Sarto, a follower who, at need, inspired himself from Raphael as well. The names put forward have been those of Puligo and Sogliani; Granacci and Franciabigio have also been suggested.

None of these names is entirely satisfactory to the discriminating eye. Franciabigio and Granacci were never quite so Raphaelesque; Puligo and Sogliani never show such charm and grace. It is true that the great cleverness of the draughtsman, with the powerful contrasts of light and shade, recall the followers of Fra Bartolommeo, and the Child's face suggests the same master; nevertheless there is something about the Cartoon, an impression as hard to define as to banish, that prevents one's thinking of it as purely Florentine. Search as we may among the painters of that school, we shall not be able to find anyone so tactful in his eclecticism, who combines and fuses with such unerring taste, the diverse influences that we have traced in this drawing. The Florentine followers of Raphael fall quickly to the low level of a Bacchiacca, who never knows how to assimilate his thefts, but makes a parade of them, like a Fiji islander, strutting about in cast-off European garments. The author of this Cartoon, on the contrary, mingles the Florentine and Raphaelesque elements, and perhaps other elements still, in such perfection that we ask : is he Raphaelesque through the traces Raphael left in Fra Bartolommeo; or does he, on the contrary, resemble the Frate through the great influence that the Frate exercised on Raphael? Still more embarrassing is it to decide whether the imperceptible aroma, which betrays a certain affinity with Leonardo, is due to an intimate and direct contact with Leonardo himself, or with one of those who continued his style, or whether the artist was imbued with it through the medium of Raphael or Fra Bartolommeo.

Who, then, can have been the author of this Cartoon? If, in the first place, he is not a Florentine, to what school does he belong, seeing that we can trace in the charming eclecticism of his style the influence of Raphael, of Fra Bartolommeo and, more

CARTOON OF THE MADONNA AND CHILD

RAPHAEL (?)

[*Miss Mackintosh.*

THE MADONNA AND CHILD

subtly, but still clearly enough, the influence of Leonardo ?

To the student really acquainted with Italian art, this question contains its own answer : the author of the British Museum drawing could not be anything but a Sienese. Towards the beginning of the sixteenth century, native Sienese art had got to such a pass that no further progress was possible without aid from the outside. It was ready to welcome anybody—and we know how, in this dearth of native talent, Sodoma came from Lombardy and overwhelmed the countryside with his paintings. One aspect of the rôle Sodoma played has, however, been but little noticed, and that is that what he really did was to introduce Florentine art to Siena and to make it popular there. Sodoma was himself—and this is the highest praise we can give him—no more than an agreeable and lucky retailer of Leonardo's inventions. Everything in them which bordered on the essential or the difficult, he omitted, being insensible to the more strenuous side of art, and by doing this he gave the Sienese exactly what, since the foundation of their school, they had always been most eager for : charming women's heads, strangely beautiful, attractive and slightly mysterious in expression, and, along with this, just enough action to make them pass muster. All this he gave them, and in a high degree of perfection : for even if it was Leonardo watered-down, it was still Leonardo! All the Sienese painters who were still young enough to be teachable, perceiving that the hour had finally struck for the old traditions of their school, traditions which nevertheless had weathered the naturalism of the fifteenth century, flocked to Sodoma's standard, and applied their talent to imitating him, or some other of the nearer and popular neighbouring artists.

Fra Paolino brought from Florence the style of his
master, Fra Bartolommeo, while Pinturicchio and
Perugino came in person, bringing their Umbrian
formulæ. At the same time Sodoma and Peruzzi,
journeying to and from Rome, ended by infusing into
Sienese painting something of Raphael, himself a
transcendent eclectic, whose style contained certain
elements not entirely foreign to their own. Meanwhile
the Sienese had begun to frequent Florentine studios.
All these various movements resulted in a most
singular fusion. As the painters of Siena had not a decided enough character of their own to hold out against
all these encroaching influences, they assimilated little
by little the styles of Fra Bartolommeo, of Raphael
and of Sodoma—all of whom, by the way, possessed
originally a good deal in common—and assimilated
them to such a point that it became almost impossible
to say under which particular influence any given work
was executed. The dominant influence, however,
was that of Fra Bartolommeo ; and this may be seen
clearly in the style of the only Sienese artist who,
in spite of the bad use he made of it, was really endowed with talent. I allude to Domenico Beccafumi.
In his figures Beccafumi often imitates Sodoma, and
sometimes Raphael, whom he may have known at
Rome ; but in his method and technique he adheres
to Fra Bartolommeo ; and never has the great Florentine artist been more closely imitated than in
Beccafumi's masterpiece, his " St. Catherine receiv-
ing the Stigmata " (Academy of Siena, X. 10).
This picture enables one to understand Vasari's en-
thusiasm for Beccafumi, whom he places above Sodoma. He has, in fact, in this work, succeeded in
catching a great deal of the Frate's sentiment; the
faces have the delicate beauty habitual to the Florentine master ; and in the landscape Beccafumi has

BECCAFUMI

ALTAR-PIECE

reproduced the exquisite opaline mist, and the clear, fathomless depth of sky that we admire in Fra Bartolommeo's "Vision of St. Bernard," and in his masterpiece at Lucca. But the side on which Beccafumi approaches him still more intimately is the brilliancy of his surfaces and his skill in the treatment of light and shade.

The fusion of styles which I have just described as one of the characteristics of the Sienese school of the sixteenth century, is precisely what we find in the British Museum drawing, combined with the delicacy, the somewhat hectic and fragile grace of the Sienese, their elusive modelling, and their contours, now hard, and now nearly invisible. It recalls above all Beccafumi, and especially the picture by him which I have just mentioned. Let us look for a moment at the upper part of this work, where the Virgin appears in glory. She is seen half-length, carrying the Child, who half stands and half kneels on her right arm ; with her left hand she gathers her mantle over her knees. The resemblance to the Madonna of our cartoon is striking. There is the same somewhat haughty rigidity of pose, almost the same grouping of the two heads, the same position and the same action of the arms. In both pictures the Child's right arm embraces his mother's neck ; in both, her left arm falls along the length of her body, and then bends inward to support the drapery below her waist. It is clear that both Beccafumi and the author of the British Museum cartoon had seen Raphael's composition of the " Vierge avec l'Enfant debout," but that the latter was so penetrated by the influence of Beccafumi that, even in copying Raphael, he could not help betraying his dependence on his Sienese master.

Who, then, is this eclectic Sienese who drew the

British Museum cartoon, if it be not Beccafumi himself? And, in the first place, why should it *not* be
Beccafumi? The objection is that the type of the
Madonna is too severe, and her beauty of too refined
a character for anything we find elsewhere in Beccafumi; she is too Florentine, and too Raphaelesque.
At the same time, the technique of the cartoon—
the black chalk and the treatment of light and shade
—is too near to Fra Bartolommeo. There remains
but one artist to suggest, a painter whose works are
not rare, but who, before Milanesi and Morelli had
rescued his name from oblivion, was almost unknown,
his pictures regularly passing under more celebrated
names. This artist is Andrea del Brescianino. Before going further, let us see what the different
authorities say of him, and under what names his
pictures have been catalogued. This inquiry will
lead us toward our end. In the catalogue of the
Munich Gallery, Brescianino is described as an imitator of Sodoma and Fra Bartolommeo; the Berlin
catalogue, on this point, entirely agrees with the one
of Munich. Herr Habich makes him a pupil of
Beccafumi, and then an imitator of Fra Bartolommeo.
And, as a matter of fact, most of his works pass
under one or the other of these two names. In the
Turin Academy, for instance, one of his Madonnas
(No. 133) is labelled "Copy after Fra Bartolommeo."
But he lends himself to other false attributions;
thus, at Glasgow, an "Adoration of the Magi" by
him (No. 15A) bears the name of Bacchiacca. The
"Madonna" at Munich leaves MM. Crowe and Cavalcaselle halting between Brescianino, and some
eclectic Florentine, such as Puligo, or Michele di
Ridolfo. We have had no occasion, so far, to bring
in the name of Raphael, but we can furnish no
better proof of the close relation between the styles

THE MADONNA AND CHILD

of Brescianino and Raphael, than the observation made by the author of the Munich catalogue in regard to Brescianino's "Madonna" there. He remarks that it is, in fact, an adaptation of the "Madonna del Baldachino" (in the Pitti). We are thus well prepared to find that the cartoon in the British Museum is an adaptation of another "Madonna" of Raphael.

Our inquiry into the artistic origin of Brescianino, as well as the examination of the names that have been given to his works, suggests nothing against the possibility of his having been the author of the British Museum cartoon. But was it actually he? I am convinced that it was. I trace those precise elements which, united and combined in this exact proportion, are not met with in any other artist. Unhappily I cannot convince my readers as I myself am convinced, for it is scarcely likely that many of them will have had enough interest in so minor a painter as to have carefully studied his evolution. The two works, however, here reproduced will indicate to them some of the steps by which I have arrived at my opinion. I reproduce the Munich "Holy Family" first, not because it is the best document in support of my attribution, but because it is a fair specimen of Brescianino at his average. A brief comparison of this work with the British Museum cartoon will not weaken my hypothesis. In both, the line of the cheek is at the same time hard and timid; in both the eyelids are vague, giving to the whole face a rather sweet expression; the nose, somewhat accentuated towards the tip, is nevertheless not very precisely indicated. The mouths are identical, each one with a big touch of shade under the lower lip. But what is still more decisive is the right hand of the Madonna in both

works.   Its outline describes a curve from the wrist
to the fingers, and its form is almost an absolute
oval.   A further significant detail is that the thumb,
hardly indicated, is barely distinguishable from the
index finger, and is lost in the same mass with it.
A detail so peculiar and unusual, added to other
favouring indications, is, in my opinion, absolutely
decisive.   The Uffizi " Madonna, Saints and Angels "
(No. 1205*bis*) is a somewhat more ambitious and
more successful work, and therefore comes nearer to
the cartoon, where, having nothing to do but to
copy an excellent model, Brescianino rises to his
highest.   I shall not insult the reader's intelligence
by drawing his attention to detail.   It will suffice to
point out the striking resemblance between the
Madonna of the drawing and the angel on the
extreme right in the altar-piece, between the heads
of the two children and the expression in all the
faces.

Since the above was written, my friend, Mr.
Herbert Cook, has published in the " Gazette des
Beaux Arts " (Troisième Période, tome xxiii., p. 410)
a version of Raphael's " Vierge avec l'Enfant debout,"
belonging to Miss Macintosh of London,[1] which,
through his kindness, I am able to reproduce.   Without discussing how much of this picture came from
Raphael's own hand, and whether a more authentic
version ever existed, it certainly is the least un-
worthy of the master among all the versions known
to me.   It is interesting, therefore, to compare the
cartoon with the painting.   The first thing that
strikes us is that this cartoon could not possibly have

[1] Exhibited in Winter Exhibition, Burlington House, 1902,
No. 82.

Anderson photo.]

[Uffizi, Florence.

THE VIRGIN AND CHILD, WITH SAINTS

served for the painting. Not only is the difference in spirit and expression considerable, not only are they of entirely different quality, but there are endless quantitative variations as well. Thus, in the picture, the oval is much more delicate, whereas in the cartoon, as in Brescianino's other pictures, it is broader and fuller. In the cartoon the Madonna's right hand has not at all the same form as in the picture, and her left, instead of holding the Child, grasps her drapery, as in Beccafumi's picture. Most striking of all is the bareness of the sleeve in the cartoon contrasted with the ample draping in the picture.

The more one compares Miss Macintosh's version of the "Vierge avec l'Enfant debout" with the British Museum cartoon, the more clearly one realizes that they are not by the same hand; whereas, the more one studies the drawing in connection with the paintings of Brescianino, the stronger must grow one's conviction that he, and he only, could have been its author.

THE DRAWINGS OF ANDREA MANTEGNA

THE painted masterpieces of Andrea Mantegna discover a feeling for line, which leads one to suspect that, casting aside the coarseness of the brush, Andrea would attain his subtlest effects in drawings with pen, pencil, or silver-point. I will not say that this expectation is wholly disappointed, for it is not; its fulfilment, however, is not found where we should have looked for it. The inevitable speed and the unfailing precision of line, which we encounter in almost any of Mantegna's well-preserved paintings, are not the qualities which we find in his drawings. In these Mantegna is, in fact, more pictorial than in his pictures; and he is more pictorial in swift, unstudied sketches than in carefully wrought-out cartoons. His first thoughts are those of an artist who perceives form in masses and not in outlines—therein betraying his affinity with the Venetians and with all born painters.

Mantegna is thus very different from the Florentines, particularly from the two great painters with whom in the past he has been frequently confounded, Antonio Pollaiuolo and Sandro Botticelli. These were in the first place linealists; and their freshest thoughts flashed before them as effects in pure line, wherein mass was not clearly indicated, but left to be inferred; while their colour, although it often ended by being exquisite, came by way of ornament to a design already complete. Effects of mass and colour were obtained by Botticelli precisely as effects of line were obtained by Mantegna—they came not as the unsought expression of a native energy, but as the spoils of hard-fought battles. The less arduous, then, the attempt, and the more freely Mantegna manifested his native power, the less do we find him winning those triumphs of line, which he earned in his more carefully executed compositions. Proceeding from his most unlaboured drawings to his most elaborately coloured canvases, we can establish a ratio of effort to effect which would sound like this : The slighter the effort, the greater the effect of mass ; the stronger the effort, the greater the effect of line.

It is possible that, in his earlier years, Mantegna was so dominated by his ideal of swift yet strenuous line, that his spontaneous bent for mass completely disappeared before it, not venturing to show itself in even the most unpretending sketch. This is possible, I say, and a certain support for such a belief will appear later. But by an accident as singular as it is unfortunate, nearly all the drawings by Mantegna that have been wafted down to us through destroying centuries, all date from his later, and even his latest years.

I

These waifs are not many, if we single out the genuine from the spurious ; but a criticism at once competent and cautious will scarcely refuse the title of authenticity to the following drawings :

CHATSWORTH. Collection of the Duke of Devonshire. Sketch for the engraving representing a

"Combat of Marine Deities." (Sepia ink on white paper. H., 24½ cm. W., 35½ cm. Photo. Braun, No. 192.)

FLORENCE. Uffizi. No. 404, Cornice 295. "Judith." (Sepia ink on washed paper, originally white. H., 36 cm. W., 24 cm. Photo. Braun, No. 191.) Signed along the right margin in those beautiful square letters the introduction of which we owe largely to Mantegna, one letter over another, with an occasional ivy leaf daintily interposed : ANDREAS MANTINIA MCCCCLXXXXI FEBI)

LONDON. British Museum. "Madonna enthroned with an Angel at her feet." (Sepia ink on brown paper. H., 19½ cm. W., 14 cm. Photo. Braun, No. 57.)

"Dying Man reclining on a stone slab." (Sepia ink on brownish paper. H., 19 cm. W., 13½ cm. Photo. Braun, No. 56.) Apparently for the famous Pietà in the Brera.

"Mars, Venus and Diana." (Outline in brown ink, shading in sepia wash and white, but touched up with ultramarine and lake; on brown paper. H., 35½ cm. W., 31½ cm. Photo. Braun, No. 58.)

"Allegory of Folly," or perhaps, "Calumny of Apelles." (Background dark reddish brown, figures light brown wash heightened with white. Woman, sphinx to left, and fire heightened with red ; ribbon entirely red. Below, to left, the monogram ΛΛ. H., 28½ cm. W., 44 cm. Photo. Braun, No. 59.)

DUBLIN, NATIONAL GALLERY. "Judith." (Grisaille, on canvas. H., 35½ cm. W., 26 cm.)

MUNICH PRINT ROOM. "A Muse." Sketch for one of the figures in the "Parnassus" of the Louvre. (Sepia, heightened with white, on brown paper. 526 × 260 mm.)

"Mucius Scaevola." (Grisaille.)

" Christ between Andrew and Longinus." Study for engraving of same subject. (Pen and ink on white paper.)

PARIS. LOUVRE. " The Judgment of Solomon." (Grisaille, on linen ; background slightly coloured. 466 × 370 mm. Photo. Braun, No. 408.)

It need scarcely be said that the eleven drawings here enumerated are not the only ones ascribed to Mantegna. Many of the ample remainder we shall meet while studying other masters ; some are copies of favourite originals like the " Judith " of the Uffizi. One copy so certainly is of an original now lost that it merits special mention. It is a sepia drawing exhibited at the museum of the Ecole des Beaux Arts in Paris, and represents the " Descent of Christ to the Shades." In all but quality this puerile production corresponds with Mantegna's engraving of the same subject. In Ridolfi's day the original of this drawing, or perchance this example itself, was in the possession of the Venetian Inquisitor, Anselmo Bresciano.[1]

The list of Mantegna's drawings would be lengthened, if we chose to include among them the master's other uncoloured works, such as the " Triumph of Scipio." This and the " Samson " have as much a place among drawings as the " Judgment of Solomon " or the " Mucius Scaevola." But in the National Gallery both are placed along with the paintings ; and, as they have nothing new to teach us, either by way of technique or touch, there we shall let them remain.

[1] Ridolfi, " Meraviglie," i. 72.

II

Pen and ink; pen, ink and sepia-wash, sepia, white lead and touches of colour; finally, grisaille with slight application of colour,—these are all the varieties of technique that we find in Mantegna's drawings.

If we now look carefully at each of the more important of these productions, we shall find, as I have already said, that, on the whole, the simpler and less studied the sketch—in other words, the more spontaneous it is—the more effective will be its manifestation of mass, and the less noteworthy its quality of line. Let us begin with the simplest drawings to end with the more elaborate.

As simple as any is the "Madonna" of the British Museum. It happens to be the earliest also, dating from Mantegna's middle period, and not, like all the other drawings, from his later years.[1] For the technique it is in, it is somewhat stiff and laboured, leading one to suspect that at the time of its execution Mantegna dared not yet allow himself liberties. But we need only hold this little sketch at a certain distance from the eye to perceive its essential features. General effect of mass, scarcely surpassable plastic values, muscular realization of movement, proper emphasis on points of force—such are

[1] The Child is of the type that we find in such a characteristic work of Mantegna's middle period as Mr. Mond's "Holy Family." The Madonna's right hand is long and slim—the hand Mantegna has in common with the young Giambellino—like the hand of the young woman in the "Circumcision" of the Uffizi triptych. The Madonna's left hand, with its thick fingers, is like the hand of the old Magian in the same triptych, and like the hand of the Madonna in a work even earlier, the San Zeno altar-piece of 1458.

ANDREA MANTEGNA

THE MADONNA AND CHILD

the marked traits of this drawing. The technique is
one aiming at light and shade alone, and the line is
completely subdued to this end. Look at any line.
It scarcely exists by itself. It is a series of meeting-
points between a mass of light and a mass of shade.
It wavers, it vanishes, it gains body and grows
puissant, the humble and always helpful ministrant
to the plastic effect. Look at the thick line—if indeed we may not more correctly call it dense shadow
—outlining the right hand: we feel even more fully
what we cannot see, the inside of wrist, palm and
fingers, than what we actually behold, the outside.
How pictorial is the depth of dense shade severing
the Madonna's cheek from the Child's head and
shoulders, or his leg from her mantle! Here also
we are compelled to an even keener realization of
the unseen than of the visible. Note how the
masses of shadow along the legs and the torso, and
the flashes of light on the knees and the shoulder,
give us the exact visual equivalents of the various
actual projections. Observe the curls escaping from
under the Madonna's kerchief, and see how the
simple touches of light and shade convey the effect,
not only of their mass, but also of their movement.
Holding it always at the same distance, look again
and note how the shadow separating the Child's left
foot from his leg makes you realize the ripple of his
chubby flesh, and the pressure as well, borne by the
ankle-joint supporting his whole body. Look once
again and see the dashing lines in the Madonna's
mantle, and note how each, serving its double purpose, indicates the firm frame of flesh and bone
beneath, and the pull of the tight-drawn drapery.
Thus might one wander over every detail of this
small sketch, and account for its function in producing the full pictorial effect. Never a link of line

for mere love of line, as among the Florentines, or
for an ideal of line, as in Mantegna's own more
elaborated achievements.

The reader would weary, if I were to make an
equally minute analysis of each and all of Mantegna's
authentic drawings.   Nor is it necessary.   The
qualities with which we have made acquaintance in
the " Madonna " we shall find unfailingly in other
sketches of equally simple means.   We should
note however that, as time went on, Mantegna
learned to allow himself a looser rein than he holds
here.

How loose a rein he could permit himself, and
how justified by an all-saving sense for mass and
plastic effect, we shall see if we stop a moment over
his cartoon for the engraving of the " Marine Combat."   In this, his least elaborated drawing, which
he seems to have executed with the greatest ease
and the least thought of outline, Mantegna is in an
unusual degree pictorial, plastic and life-communicating.   We have here also the fullest roundness of
relief; and, in addition, a rare effect of circumfused
air and water unifying the composition atmo-
spherically.   At the same time, the fire and spirit of
the sea-horses, and the energy of the onset, sweep
us out into the tide of their fierce life.

Much of this fire evaporated with attention to line
for its own sake, as we shall readily perceive in
comparing this cartoon with the finished engraving.
The engraving is not so plastic, the atmospheric
effect has disappeared, and, with it, the pictorial
charm.   What the line has gained in continuity, it
certainly has lost in life and force.   Whither has the
spirit fled from the horses?   You could hear them
neigh and champ.   It was a pleasure to pat their
beautiful heads.   The toss of their manes made the

ANDREA MANTEGNA

THE BATTLE OF THE MARINE GODS

air electric. How tame all this has grown in the engraving!

Yet one other sketch in the simple technique of sepia demands attention. It is a drawing lacking none of the qualities which make the cartoon for the " Combat " delightful, and at the same time possessing attractiveness and power as a masterly rendering of a great theme—I refer to the " Judith " in the Uffizi.

Twice, and perhaps thrice, has Mantegna treated this subject; twice without colour, and once as a painting. Whatever point of view we choose to start from; whether we regard the specifically artistic effect, or the presentation of spiritual significance, we shall agree, I believe, in preferring the " Judith " of the Uffizi to the one in grisaille formerly belonging to Col. Malcolm, and now at Dublin; or to the doubtful one in Lord Pembroke's collection, painted in tempera, and finished with the mincing primness and the niggling precision of a miniature.

We all know the story of Judith. She soothes her people's enemy into a besotted sleep, and while he sleeps she cuts off his head. She has played her part well, caressing and cajoling, with mortal hatred and deadly determination at her heart; and now at last, after such tension, her fever-strung nerves relax, and she gives way to her pent-up feelings.

In every version of the story, this is the moment which Mantegna has chosen to depict. The earliest certainly, if really by Andrea, is Lord Pembroke's tempera painting, treated, as I have already said, laboriously and minutely. All that we see is modelled with cautious care; the relief is full and round; but the figures do not escape Squarcione's taunt—they suggest marble rather than flesh and blood. A perfectly plastic figure should be so modelled, that we realize the unseen parts of it as vividly as the visible. Such modelling we found in the "Madonna" of the British Museum, and in the Duke of Devonshire's "Marine Combat." In Lord Pembroke's "Judith," the contours are coast-lines enislanding the figures. In his pre-occupation over the lineal effect, Mantegna, if indeed it was he, seems to have forgotten what he had started to do ; and has given but a sorry interpreta-tion of his theme. Judith holds the gory head in her hand, but she feels neither hatred nor exultation. She shows the face of Faustina, morose with the lassitude of a disappointing orgie.

Such is Lord Pembroke's painting. And now look at the Uffizi drawing. This Judith is no Roman empress of the decline. She presents a slim figure, majestically tall, a profile of Athene, such as Hellenic genius at its height conceived. From head to foot her tremulous frame is quivering with loath-ing ; and for disgust her fingers will scarcely touch the hated head.

The specifically artistic qualities of this work are worthy of the interpretation. The means used are as simple as in the "Marine Combat." With sepia on white paper, Mantegna attains effects of unsur-passable plasticity, of resplendent colour. Note, for instance, how white and round the right arm emerges from the impenetrable blackness. But let us hear what Messer Giorgio Vasari has to say touching this masterpiece :

"There is in our portfolio, on a half sheet royal, a drawing by Andrea of a Judith putting in the bag of a negress slave the head of Holofernes. It is in black and white, but of a technique no longer prac-tised ; for in place of white lead, he has used the white ground so skilfully that you see the separate

[*Uffizi, Florence.*

JUDITH WITH THE HEAD OF HOLOFERNES

hairs spun out, and such other refinements, as if they had been done most daintily with a brush. Wherefore this sheet may be regarded as a painting rather than as a drawing."[1]

III

With the sepia version of the Uffizi, the Dublin "Judith" may not be compared, either for interpretation or execution. It is the ablest of Mantegna's works in grisaille, his most elaborate technique ; but we quickly note the hampering of energy both mental and manual. No fierce rebound from stifling oppression is depicted here, but the self-pity and lassitude of one tasting the futility of revenge, and foreseeing further wrongs.

The modelling is more obvious than in the sepia sketch, but scarcely so plastic ; with one exception, the touch is never so vivifying. The hair of Holofernes is the exception, the locks of which are like swaying river grasses swept by the wind. But Judith's own hair, somewhat limp, and mechanically curled, lacks the life-communicating quality of the Uffizi drawing. Taken by itself, however, the

[1] Vasari, Sansoni, iii. 402. Doubts have been cast upon the identity of the Uffizi drawing with the one described by Vasari. He expressly states—and it is his point—that the drawing shows the white of the sheet where most artists would have used white lead. The Uffizi drawing, however, is touched up with white lead. But a careful scrutiny will soon convince one that these touches are each and all relatively recent. They never add to the effect, but generally detract from it, often carelessly going over the blacks, and always looking fresher than the rest of the surface. Granting, as every competent critic will, that the white is a later addition, Vasari's description perfectly fits the Uffizi "Judith"—nay more than fits, is a most illuminating criticism.

Dublin Judith is one of the masterpieces of Italian art, as composition, as arrangement, as modelling, as movement, to be surpassed only by Mantegna himself. It suffers somewhat beside the more spontaneously felt and simply executed sketch; but gains vastly when confronted with any other of Mantegna's drawings equally elaborate.

But first I would draw attention to a quality which the Dublin grisaille possesses in an eminent degree, the quality of line. Look at the swift, unswerving lines of Judith's draperies. Some of them have the flow of silent streams. You will not find such lineal perfection in the sepia drawings. There, as I have said, the effort was less, and the effect of mass and colour greater; here, there is more labour, and a closer approach to Mantegna's conscious ideal, surety of line.

Passing over the powerfully conceived and ably executed, but now somewhat washed-out " Mucius Scaevola "[1] of Munich, let us look at the elaborate grisaille of the Louvre, representing the " Judgment of Solomon." Were it not for the subject, we behold what we easily might mistake for the copy of a bas-relief from the age of the Antonines. The conception is tame, almost cheap, the execution careful and cold. There is no effect of mass, no grouping and fusing atmosphere. The figures stand like stiff statuary, unkindled and unkindling. The executioners are ignoble gladiators, and the child's real mother is their mate. Neither values of plasticity nor of force are accentuated. How merely mask-like are

---

[1] This can scarcely be other than the work seen in 1512 by the Anonimo Morelliano in the house of Francesco Zio, and thus entered: "El quadretto de Muzio Scevola che brusa la mano propria, finto da bronzo, fu de mano de Andrea Mantegna." Edition Frizzoni, p. 179.

JUDITH WITH THE HEAD OF HOLOFERNES

most of the faces! How little life there is in any
joint! On the other hand, the contours are clean
and precise, and the line by itself has great beauty.
Note the hair of the executioners, and the lineal
effect of the young guard's entire figure.

IV

Between the boldly spontaneous sepia sketches
and the over-elaborated grisailles, not quite rising to
the vivacity of the first, nor sinking to the tameness
of the others, the three drawings of mixed technique
find their fit place.   One of them, the " Mars, Venus
and Diana," almost wholly in sepia, is less elaborate
than the other two, and has many of the qualities of
the least laboured works.   The " Muse " and the
" Allegory " are highly and cautiously finished, but
artistically no less valuable.

All three may be connected with the paintings
Mantegna furnished soon after 1490 for the study of
his fascinating patroness, Isabella d'Este, Mar-
chioness of Mantua.   The " Venus, Mars and Diana "
may have been a first thought for the group of Mars
and Venus upon the hillock in the " Parnassus."
The " Muse " was certainly for the same picture,
and Mantegna transferred her figure to the canvas
with scarcely a change.[1]   The " Allegory " is a
sketch for a picture that seems never to have been

[1] The face in the painting is significantly different, and has the
individualized traits of a portrait, and not Mantegna's usual type,
which appears in the drawing.   Having sketched, for the action,
this foremost of the muses, Mantegna, in transferring it to canvas,
added a portrait face.   It will be noted that this is the only face
in comparative repose, and looking out of the picture.   I venture
to believe that the portrait is of no other than Isabella herself.

painted, having probably given place to the kindred subject of the " Expulsion of the Vices."

The first of these, the " Mars, Venus and Diana," is almost entirely in sepia, and although much more studiously finished than Mantegna's other drawings in this technique, partakes of their freedom, plasticity and suggestiveness. The modelling of the Diana is peculiarly appealing.[1]

The successful search for subtile line has, it is true, resulted in exquisite contours, but there is a loss of force values. The hands are hardly prehensile ; the joints communicate but feeble pressures to one another ; the limbs do not weigh their full weight.

The " Muse " is masterly in modelling and in movement of line. Perhaps we should consider this drawing chiefly as a study of drapery. As such it lacks little of perfection. How the folds flutter as she dances ; and yet they mould the form under them, the breasts, the waist, the hips, each with its utmost plasticity ! Apply the test from which masterpieces alone emerge : imagine this sheet torn to tatters ; like fragments of great Greek art, every shred would betray its value and function, conjuring up the whole.

The " Allegory " is as elaborate in execution as it is enigmatical in intention. Is the king in his bloated nakedness esconced on a globe kept firm by sphinzes, Emperor of the Fools, or is he Midas ? Is the hag beside him Envy, and the bandaged maid Justice ? And what may be the meaning of the

[1] She has been transferred with but little change of action to the "Parnassus," where, however, she figures as Venus. Drapery and head apart, the Venus here is in figure and movement almost identical with the Uffizi " Judith," which, as we remember, is dated 1491.

ANDREA MANTEGNA

DRAWING OF A MUSE

other group : the nude girl about to leap over the precipitous wall ; the dancing faun ; the piping satyr, and the uncanny figure led by a crawling dog, his own head wrapped in a handkerchief tied around his neck, as we tie a rag over a stopper? He of course is Blindness ; but what does it all signify ?[1]

Fortunately our purpose is not the guessing of charades, but the appreciation of the work of art, and as a work of art the " Allegory" is not obscure. To judge it at its full value we should regard it not as the hot transcript of a dazzling idea, but as a work finished even to the finger-nail ; whereupon it takes rank among Mantegna's masterpieces. The firmness of the modelling, the loading of the limbs, the pressure upon the joints, are one and all directly force-communicating. Much is here sacrificed to contour; but the beauty of the outlines almost weans one from that fusion of form and atmosphere, those effects of mass and colour, in a word, from that higher plasticity which we found in the " Judith," and in the other unelaborated drawings by Mantegna.

[1] An engraving exists in which this drawing is faithfully reproduced, and continued below, where a dungeon appears.

A WORD FOR RENAISSANCE
CHURCHES

SPONTANEOUS feeling for art is a gift possessed by few. Most of us enjoy works of art indirectly, by association, by preparation, and, above all, by finding in them what our education and general reading have led us to expect. How many good people of every possible shade of belief or unbelief manage to miss the point in Italian galleries, and come away scornful and disgusted because they have not found in a single picture either their own ideal of the Madonna, or the ideal they consider a Christian ought to have! Even those, however, who would think it crude to look for nothing in a Madonna but a type of woman worthy to be the Mother of God, are nevertheless proud of advertising their contempt for the Italian churches of the Renaissance "because they are not religious." Let it at once be freely granted that Renaissance churches do not evoke that sense of awe and mystery, which the mediæval Christian is supposed to have felt in his places of worship. Does that necessarily condemn them? In this sense no one dreams of calling the Parthenon or the Theseum, the Temples of Girgenti or Segesta, religious; yet everyone enjoys and admires them. And it would be as absurd to defeat our power of enjoying the beautiful architecture of Renaissance churches, on the score that they are not in this sense religious, as it would be to put all Titian's and

Tintoretto's glorious Madonnas out of court, because they do not happen to express any of our ideals of the Virgin.

In Italy religion has never been what it has been elsewhere in Europe. Italy invented all the forms, all the machinery of mediæval Christianity; but the Italians, as a people, never felt and never sympathized with the spirit which the North poured into the forms they had invented. Italy remained pagan and classical even in Christianity. She insisted upon subordinating the whole of existence to a scheme. She parcelled out the universe, leaving no room for vague emotions, or for the sense of mystery. The Italian people may be likened to the prince of the fairy tale who did not know what it was to shiver. They never knew what it was to have that feeling of mystery which haunted the North, that sense of being in the presence of unknowable and unimaginable, though almost tangible, powers. Lacking this feeling, their art lacks it. Their literature has no touch of weirdness; their painting, if it has magic at all, has only the sunflooded magic of a midsummer day. Their architecture has nothing awe-inspiring about it. But awe and mystery are what the northern mind of to-day chiefly demands in the churches of the past; and as the churches of the Renaissance are wholly without awe and mystery, the northern mind, with something of that rudeness indicative of its barbarous origin, is apt to dismiss them all.

Is it possible that the Italian people, supreme in all the other arts, and unrivalled as builders of palaces, should have made a failure of it when they undertook to build churches? This is, on the face of it, unlikely. They were, in truth, quite as successful in church architecture as in every other form of art. Our inability to appreciate this comes from the fact that their success is of another kind from that of Gothic builders, because their ideal was of an altogether different sort from the northern. The northern artist strove to express his own feeling of awe, and to impose it on others. The Italian thought of nothing but perfect space, proportion, and order.

In this, he resembled his Roman ancestors. Purists say that Roman architecture was fundamentally bad, because it masked the essential fabric with orders unnecessary to the structure. But purists forget that what the Roman architect sought was to express the majesty and grandeur of Rome. The more the Romans themselves became aware of the splendour of their empire, the more their architects endeavoured to express it in building. As a people naturally attains to full consciousness of its greatness only when that greatness has passed its zenith, Roman architecture was most magnificent as the Empire began to wane and totter. No buildings now remaining in Rome produce such an overwhelming impression as the later edifices, such as the Baths of Caracalla, and the Basilica of Constantine. The colossal scale and the massiveness of the masonry at first crowd out every other impression. But when you begin to ask what these halls could have been as enclosures, you realize that they must have been symphonies of space, producing on the senses the tonic and ennobling effect of classical music. This symphonic effect we miss in the ruins because they have been stripped of the orders, the cornices, the columns, the niches—the purist's stumbling-blocks!—none of which, it is true, were necessary to the structure, though all were essential to the life, vivacity, and harmonious effect.

What was true of the Romans was no less true of their descendants. The Italian architect never ceased to strive for a perfect effect of space. No matter what may be said against the great Christian basilicas of Rome, no one can fail to be struck by their noble spaciousness. The same quality characterizes all Italian churches, even in the darkest periods of mediævalism. In Lombardy there was perhaps a momentary wavering toward a Teutonic ideal, but never in Central Italy. The cathedral of Pisa is an excellent instance of a mediæval yet spacious Italian church. Compared with the best specimens of northern Romanesque, the interior of Pisa lacks in gravity. It is less like a Gregorian chant. But how freely one breathes there! The eye glides easily from column to column, to find its rest in the apse, instead of having to hop from pillar to pillar, before plunging into an obscure choir. The nave, to which the aisles are completely subordinated, is spacious and airy. Or take the cathedral of Orvieto, with its simple and dignified interior. It was put up by architects from Siena, a town where painting had almost a northern depth of religious feeling. Yet the interior of Orvieto is not specifically religious. As you look from the aisle to the row of windows piercing the wall upborne by imposing arches, you are irresistibly reminded of the façade of some splendid palace of the early Renaissance. When they became architects, even the townsmen and contemporaries of Simone Martini, and the Lorenzetti, the most Gothic in spirit of all the Italian artists, had to submit to the law that governed Italian architecture, and to strive for an effect of space rather than for an impression of awe. The Franciscan Order itself only encouraged this natural tendency by its preference for churches consisting of

a wide nave with no aisles at all.   To the eye
expecting the magic of Amiens or Westminster, a
church like Santa Croce at Florence can seem little
else than a barn.   But as an effect of space and
harmony produced by the simplest conceivable
means, Santa Croce has few rivals.   All these
churches prove that Italian architecture, to put it
shortly, was no less controlled by the memory of
Roman space effects, than Italian politics was shaped
by the memory of the Roman empire.

The Renaissance, then, even in church building,
marks no such break with the past as is often supposed.   The Italian of the Renaissance was not
essentially a different being from the Italian of the
Middle Ages.   He differed from his great grand-
fathers chiefly by being much more conscious of his
aims.   The Renaissance architect was well aware
that an effect of space and proportion was the principal aim of his art; and it was this that led him to
turn his most loving study to the construction of
domed churches on the plan of a Greek cross; for
no architectural form can realize a sense of space to
such a degree as a dome resting on grand arches.
Long before the fifteenth century this had been felt.
Pisa has a dome, Ancona has one, both from the
twelfth century; Siena has one of a kind, Bologna
was to have had one, and Florence has the greatest
in existence.   Brunelleschi's dome, finished in 1436,
was the first great achievement of Renaissance
architecture; but it must be borne in mind that if
the achievement was Brunelleschi's, the problem was
much older than the artist.   There was, however,
this difference.   To the fourteenth century architects
the dome was the crowning point, but to Brunelleschi
it was the building itself.   At Florence stand at the
corner of the Via del Proconsolo, where you see

nothing of the cathedral but Brunelleschi's dome rising over the short choir and transepts. Does it look merely like the crowning point of a great edifice ? Not at all. You see and feel nothing but the dome, and this so dominates you that you scarcely notice the childishness of the barber-pole marble casing of the walls. From this point walk on until you come in full sight of the nave and Giotto's Tower. Both, splendid as they are in themselves, seem impertinent beside the dome. You cannot forgive the nave for shutting out the view of the dome from the façade, and the tower seems to have no place in such company. When you have fallen under the spell of that vast dome you abhor everything that comes in its way. If the modern Florentines had dared to make the most of a splendid opportunity, they would have cut the nave short, and put on a modest façade as a prelude to the dome, instead of that clever anthology of Italian cemetery sculpture which, under the specious name of façade, now irretrievably hides it.

The Italian architects of the fourteenth century, although they felt that no other form could give effects of space equal to those given by a dome, were only dimly conscious of their purpose, and seemed unaware of the flagrant contradiction between dome and nave, the one drawing the eye upwards, the other directing it, along a vista of pillars, to the apse. In the fifteenth century, however, Brunelleschi, conscious at last of the real purpose of the dome, sought to get rid of the contradiction the moment he had a free hand, by erecting a cupola upon a cruciform structure with arms of equal length.

The reason for the choice of this special cruciform shape, is that no architectural form so completely composes space into a harmony as a dome on arches.

These arches, if they are to convey the complete effect of the interior at the first glance, must be each of a certain equal depth. If the arches are not deep enough the eye runs straight across to the apse, missing, at the first glance, the dome. If the arches, on the other hand, are too deep—that is, if they are so deep as to interfere with the complete effect of the interior, dome as well as arches, the plan is absurd. The extra depth is useless, considering that the aim is to produce a single impression of perfect space. But arches of more than adequate depth are worse than useless; they are a positive evil. As you enter you cannot help seizing the effect of what seems the whole of the interior. Now if the arches supporting the dome are so deep that your first impression does not include the dome, as soon as you discover that the dome, and not the deep arches you saw on entering, is the real point, there is a struggle in your mind between the two impressions. It ends in the triumph of the second impression, the impression of the dome, but meanwhile the feeling of harmony has been disturbed.

This, then, was the problem of the Renaissance architect, and this explains the passion he had for the domed church in the form of a Greek cross. The church had to be domed because the perfection of space can be attained only by the meeting of four arches under a dome. It had to be cruciform, with arches of equal depth, so that from whatever point you entered you at once received the complete effect of the interior.

The Pazzi Chapel in Florence is the first realization of a problem, that, for a hundred and fifty years, continued to be the master problem of Italian architecture. What Brunelleschi began, Alberti, the San Gallo, Bramante, Michelangelo, and a hundred less

celebrated architects, continued—the purpose becoming more and more consciously an effect of perfect space, proportion, and order. They took space
for a language as the musician takes sound. They
strove to produce an effect that would make one on
entering a church feel the existence of space as a
positive fact, instead of a mere negation of solidity ;
as a material, not a void ; and, beyond this, as a
material capable of being shaped in the subtlest
fashion. The moment you enter such a church as
the Madonna della Consolazione at Todi—the best,
although far from perfect, realization of the Renaissance ideal—you feel as if you had cut loose from
gravitation, and as if you took flight not only from
the material universe, but also from all that is your
conscious self. The builder of such a church makes
space no less eloquent than a composer makes sound.
An Italian architect is really a space-composer.

The perfect realization of this ideal was to have
been St. Peter's ; and if the original plans had been
carried out, it would have been the very greatest
achievement in all art. But that the greatest work
of art in the world should have been the Metropolitan
Temple of Catholicism, would have been against all
the laws that govern human expression, considering
that the Church as such had never loved, but merely
suffered and exploited art. So St. Peter's was not
completed in accordance with Bramante's design.
What makes the church at Todi the most interesting
church of the Renaissance, is the fact that, on a
small and meagre scale, it comes nearest to the
original scheme for St. Peter's. I do not mean to
imply that it was copied from Bramante's designs, or
that the Todi architect was in any way acquainted
with Bramante. Bramante's plan would have been
merely the perfect realization of that striving for an

effect of space which animated the Roman architect,
was never given up by the Italian of the Middle
Ages, and was resumed with passionate eagerness
by all the architects of the Renaissance ; and as this
architectural ideal was in Italy more national and universal than even Gothic had been in France, many
Italian architects gave it independent expression.
The various expressions cluster about Bramante's
plans for St. Peter's, not because they are derived
from these plans, but because they are all tending
toward the same thing ; and they approach Bramante
in the measure of their success, the church at Todi
coming nearest to him, because it is the best realization of the Italian ideal of space.   Unfortunately it
was not finished at once, so that the pilasters and
cornices fail to give that rhythmical effect one finds
in the Pazzi Chapel, or in San Gallo's masterpiece,
the Madonna delle Carcere at Prato.   But the bad
detail does not spoil the marvellous effect of the
whole.   Mr. Ruskin with his golden pen might have
re-created this interior for us in splendid periods, had
he not wasted himself on far-fetched enthusiasms
begot of neo-Catholic sentimentality.   As it is, we
must wait for a critic with equal rhetorical power but
larger sympathies.

One has to be inside the church for some time
before the thought occurs that the purpose of the
building was other than the realization of a beautiful
dream of space.   It suggests no ulterior motive.   It
is sufficient in itself.   Recovering from the first
transport and looking about, one wonders what the
altars mean, they seem so uncouthly out of place.
Such a building sings indeed not the glory of God,
but the Godhood of man, who is here a creator on a
level at least with the Mediæval Demiurge.   But
the central shrine of Catholicism could not be a

building which put man on a level with God. It could not be an edifice which intoxicated him with beauty and power and joy, as Bramante's St. Peter's would have done. Catholicism wanted in its greatest church a building that would humiliate man before its own splendour. St. Peter's was given a long nave, cased with priceless marble, that irresistibly draws the eye to the altar as the centre of interest; and as you promenade about the interior of the vast building you feel that the people who built it had bottomless purses at their disposal, and did things on a colossal scale. St. Peter's nave is admirably calculated to impress the peasant from the Abruzzi, from the Tyrol, or from Brittany, as he is led about by his parish priest. It shows him how grandly the Holy Father once lived, and incites him to bitter hatred of those who now prevent him from living in such state as befits this, his private chapel.

The chief interest of the Italian architect having been the attainment of a perfect effect of space, he concentrated his attention upon the interior. To him the outside was as nothing in comparison. This explains why so many Italian churches are completely finished in the interior, and left rough on the outside, with no attempt at a façade. In the north, on the contrary, there are comparatively few churches whose façades, if we except the towers, are not as finished as their interiors. Certain cathedrals, indeed, such as St. Denis and Notre Dame de Paris, have façades in an earlier style than the rest of the building, proving that they were actually built before the interiors. It is a temptation to parody Mr. Ruskin by scolding at the northern builders for thinking of nothing but making a show, because they sometimes began with the façade, the show-piece. But beginning with the façade is in strict accordance with the specific idea of Gothic architects. To them a building was something "a man who was really a carpenter made," a matter of carpentry and props, a carpenter-made chest on a colossal and majestic scale.[1] In Gothic, the façade is therefore almost as essential as the side of a chest which is held together by fitting notch into notch without the use of a single nail. The wonder is that in France, where Gothic is most like carpentry, they did not more frequently begin with the façade. But to the perfect effect of space, the Italian's ideal, the façade has only an indirect relation. The Italian consequently neglected it, or treated it as an independent member, frankly standing by itself, like the façade of Orvieto, an expression of that other ideal which in Italy has been subordinated only to the ideal of space,—the ideal of magnificence and splendour.

It was unfortunate that Italian architecture became aware of its ideal in an age that had no occasion for the building of Cathedral churches. Almost all the Italian Sees date from the earlier Christian centuries. Totally new cathedrals, therefore, were not built in the Renaissance. The old ones were rebuilt, and in rebuilding the architect was obliged to adhere more or less to the original plan. In such cases he made a compromise, such as Wren was obliged to make in St. Paul's, between his passion for the dome and the demand of piety for the old form of the Christian basilica. He hitched on a long nave to the domed Greek cross. It is true, furthermore, that even in Italy popular prejudice would have militated against the new form for cathedrals, or for any very important churches. Domed churches are seldom of any great size, and

[1] See M. Courajod's "Louvre Lectures."

indeed size, beyond a certain point, is of as little importance in giving a perfect effect of space as length is of importance to the beauty of a symphony. These churches seem to have been built for the pleasure of giving finish to a beautiful spot outside the town walls, and they are usually to be found standing on terraces on the slopes of hills, commanding fascinating prospects. Many instances could be mentioned, but it is enough to refer to some of the loveliest, such as S. Maria Nuova at Cortona, S. Biagio at Montepulciano, S. Maria Belvedere at Città di Castello, S. Maria delle Vergine at Macerata, and S. Bernardino at Urbino. Catholicism, in adopting the basilica for its principal churches, found a form well suited to its own purposes. In a basilica the lines firmly converge to the tribune where the judges sat. In the church the exact place of the tribune was occupied by the altar, where God was worshipped, where in the Host He was bodily present. In the vaulting of the tribune Christ was represented as the stern Judge. (It is no mere accident, for instance, that the altar wall of the Sixtine Chapel is taken up by Michelangelo's "Last Judgment.") The mediæval Christian wanted, the moment he entered a church, to direct his eyes and his heart to the point where his God dwelt, and where he was represented as Judge. To him it must have seemed next to blasphemy to be given a kind of architecture which drew his eye upward towards a dome, and obscured, almost made impossible, his view of the apse; for in a fine domed church you can no more help turning your eyes to the cupola, than you can help marching to music.

It took the temerity and military audacity of Pope Julius to raze to the ground the most venerable church in Christendom, and to begin to erect in

its place a building that would have proved how
well the Italians had forgotten mediæval Christianity,
and how completely it had given place to the worship of reason and force, which, in the new St.
Peter's, were to be embodied in perfect form. No
wonder that visitors from the north were horrified
by this idea! No wonder that, in popular history,
the building of St. Peter's is always made a principal cause of the Reformation! The north was
tired of Roman rule, and after more than fifteen
hundred years of submission to the Empire and to
its spectre, the Papacy, that part of the north which
Roman rule had least firmly rivetted to itself, broke
away. Bramante's St. Peter's, the north dimly felt,
brought it face to face with an idea even more purely
Roman, more distinctly Italian, than the Ruota
itself. It served the curious end of warning the
Teutonic peoples that the time for a complete break
with the Papacy had come, as it proved that the
Papacy had shrunk to a merely Italian institution,
no longer seriously pretending to satisfy universal
needs. The Reformation frightened the Papacy
into all sorts of pious resolutions and disgusting
hypocrisies, in its dread of going to utter ruin, and
in the hope of winning back the north. St. Peter's
was sacrified to the spirit that prevailed at the
Council of Trent. In spite of the apparent swaying
backward and forward of the architects, the long
nave was inevitable. This has reduced St. Peter's
to the most colossal failure in art, but Catholicism
was satisfied. The dome is hidden from the entrance
within and without. Yet Italian genius could not
wholly forget itself. The ideal of perfect space
simply gave way to its close although inferior com-
panion, the ideal of palatial grandeur—an ideal to
which Italians always sank on losing or sacrificing

their passion for an effect of perfect space. For-
bidden his most natural striving, the Italian architect
endeavoured to combine the best effect of space he
could attain, outside the cruciform structure, with
the imposing appearance of such palaces as the
Vatican or Farnese. The present nave of St. Peter's,
in spite of its size, does not make such an impression
of spaciousness as an old basilica like Santa Maria
Maggiore ; but, to make up for it, the nave looks
as much as possible like the *salon* of a princely
palazzo. Even the façade tries to be palatial ; and
if, in the case of St. Peter's, it does not quite succeed in looking like a palace front, in the case of
Santa Maria Maggiore the eighteenth-century fronts
might well be taken for palaces. In that century,
Italian architects retained so little sense of the
difference between a church front and any other
façade, that it would require slight alteration to
make the fronts of St. John Lateran and the Trevi
Fountain change places without incongruity. But
thereby the pagan spirit of Italy succeeded once
more in ridding itself of Christianity, and its achievements during the eighteenth century are in far better
taste than the buildings of the century previous,
when Italian genius tried to squeeze itself into a
fashion more truly opposed to its spirit than Gothic
itself. This was the Jesuit ideal of well-upholstered
cosiness, that attempt to turn a church into a boudoir,
which developed into Rococo. The interior of
St. John Lateran is a ludicrous instance of what
happened to a basilica, and the ideal of spaciousness
it expressed, when it had to put on a rococo mask.
Far from being cosy, gay, and playful, it looks
morose and heavy.

In short, the law governing Italian architecture
has always been the same, and even to-day the ideal

of space is as great an inspiration as ever.   No matter what the faults of such a building as the Glass Gallery at Milan, certainly no one will deny that it is magnificently spacious.   Italians have always succeeded when they sought to express an ideal of space, and failed whenever they attempted anything else—particularly when the attempt was something distinctly opposed to this ideal.   An understanding of this law teaches us what to look for in Renaissance churches and architecture, and prepares our minds to appreciate them.

CERTAIN UNRECOGNIZED PAINTINGS
BY MASOLINO

IT has been my good fortune in the last seven years to find several pictures which can be added to the too meagre list of Masolino's works. One is a marvellous " Annunciation " at Gosford House, the Scottish seat of Lord Wemyss ; another a Madonna in the Kunsthalle at Bremen, and, finally, there are remains of decorations for an entire hall in the Palazzo Castiglione at Castiglione d'Olona. The " Annunciation " is a large picture in which we see the lovely-faced Virgin sitting on the right, in a hall of slender columns ; while, on the left, kneels the flaxen-haired angel, dressed in a robe embroidered all over with golden roses. It is a panel of such remarkable decorative effect that it is hard to find room for it in the too narrow limits of almost colourless sobriety usually assigned to the trend of Florentine Art. Even less expected are the remains at the Palazzo Castiglione. As one may see by the frieze that runs around the whole hall, once all the four walls were frescoed. Three of them have been covered with whitewash ; but on the fourth we see a sight that conventional art-history has taught us to look for scarcely at all in the painting of the Renaissance, and least of all in Florentine art of the earlier years of the Quattrocento. What we see is nothing less than a vast landscape, a sort of Panorama of the Alps, with a broad torrent swiftly rushing down to the plain.   That its author was Masolino we are assured by the likeness in essentials to the landscape of the " Baptism " in the frescoes decorating the Baptistery of this same Lombard artistic paradise ; we are further assured by the resemblance of these mountain masses to those of Masolino's pupil, Masaccio, in the Brancacci Chapel at Florence ; further still, by the medallion heads in the frieze, unmistakably Masolino's.   And being by this master, and not later, therefore, than the fourth decade of the fifteenth century, let us cease talking nonsense about the late date at which, in Italy, landscape began to be treated on its own account. Most of the painting that has come down to us from those early years is of a sacred character, and it surely is not in sacred pictures that we should naturally look for independent treatment of landscape.   In the interior decoration of palaces it may have occurred early and frequently, but these notoriously perish easily under the needs and caprices of their inhabitants.   Very few, in fact, have escaped destruction, and this one is all the more precious.   It should warn us to give no heed to negative evidence, and to put no value on generalizations made thereon.

Masolino's " Madonna " at Bremen is a charming and highly characteristic work of that kind wherein frame and picture are one.   The Virgin sits on a cushion while the Child leaps up from her knee, to fling his arms around her neck,—a motive which is as tender as it is unusual.   In the spandril of the richly-carved flamboyant frame, is painted the head of Christ.   Below on the frame, which, be it noted, forms one inseparable whole with the picture, is an inscription with the date 1423.   This is of capital

interest, for undisputable dates in Masolino's career
are rare—so rare indeed that this one is unique.

Gladly would I speak at much greater length of
the three works so cursorily mentioned, but without
offering the reader reproductions of them, I could
not hope to interest him. For the present, then, I
must leave them, hoping to return to them when I
shall have succeeded in obtaining their photographs.
I will speak of two works which, like the three
already mentioned, have never been brought into
connection with Masolino,[1] although in my opinion
they clearly are by that fascinating artist. One is a
panel at Munich representing the Madonna (No.
1019), the other a fresco in the church of S. Ste-
fano at Empoli. Thereafter I shall take note of
a fresco in the Baptistery at Empoli, which can
safely be ascribed to the same artist.

Before going further, I must make a brief digression in explanation of the evidence I shall bring to
bear, and the method I shall pursue in attempting
to prove that these two works are by Masolino.

I shall bring into court no witness of a disputable
kind, except in one instance, that instance being the
frescoes in the Brancacci Chapel at Florence,[2] which,
in common with Frizzoni, Morelli, Richter, Wick-
hoff, and a goodly number of others, among them
Vasari himself, I would ascribe to our painter, and
not to his far greater pupil, Masaccio. Unhappily
that church-father of more recent art-studies, the
late Signor Cavalcaselle, was of a different opinion.
He pronounced that Masolino had no hand in the

---

[1] At least to my knowledge they never had, when I first published them, in the first and second edition of my "Florentine
Painters."

[2] The Brancacci frescoes have been photographed admirably
by Anderson ; those at Castiglione d'Olona by Alinari.

frescoes still remaining in the Brancacci Chapel.
Consistency drove him to this unfortunate decision ;
for, acute as his eye was, his judgment was too
timid to grapple with the errors of Vasari ; and as
Vasari ascribed the frescoes in S. Clemente at
Rome to Masaccio, Cavalcaselle, despite the clear
report of his eyes, also ascribed them to Masaccio.
Aghast at the gulf between the works given by
Messer Giorgio to Masaccio in Rome, and those in
Florence, to bridge it, he was forced to throw across
Masolino's Brancacci frescoes.   If these are Masaccio's, then certainly those at S. Clemente and the
two delightful panels at Naples are his also : and so
also in logic and candour should be the frescoes at
Castiglione d'Olona.   Unfortunately for this expan-
sive cry of *plus de frontières*, these are authenticated
as Masolino's.   Criticism has gone on promenading
comfortably over this Cavalcasellian bridge, apparently unaware of its flimsy structure.   Is its un-
trustworthiness at last beginning to be suspected by
such stout defenders of the Cavalcasellian faith as
Dr. Bode ? I see in the last edition of the " Cicerone"
that he begins to suspect that perchance Masolino,
after all, may still be seen at the Brancacci Chapel.
Let him continue this good way, and he must con-
clude that the same artist is responsible for the
frescoes in Rome, and the panels at Naples as well.
On this road there is no stopping.

The works, then, by Masolino on which I shall
draw for terms of comparison are the undisputed
ones at Castiglione d'Olona, and the still debated
frescoes in the Brancacci Chapel, especially the large
one, whose chief episode represents the " Raising of
Tabitha."   Vasari's authority and the evidence of
my eyes tell me that this work is Masolino's.   As for
Vasari it may be objected that I have no right to

MASOLINO

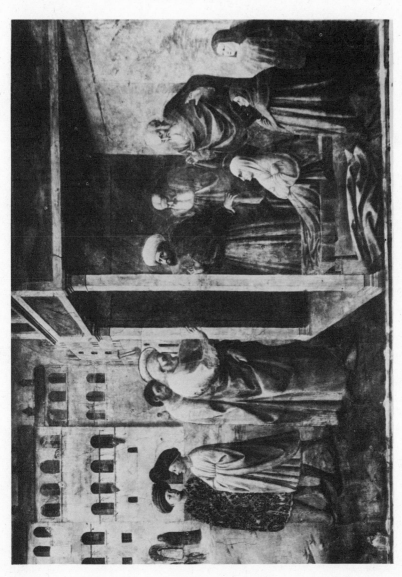

[Church of the Carmine, Florence.

THE RAISING OF TABITHA

benefit by his witness in one place, when I reject it
in the other. My reader, like the satyr in the fable,
may run away from a mouth that blows both hot and
cold. But if he has more sense than the satyr, he
will reflect that there is a time for a mouth to blow
hot and a time for it to blow cold, a time for disre-
garding Vasari, and a time for regarding him.

Vasari is to be regarded in the measure of the
probability that the tradition which he handed down
was well founded. In the present instance a sound
tradition with regard to two Florentine painters
so conspicuous as Masolino and Masaccio is much
more likely to have been perpetuated in Florence
than at Rome. The Brancacci Chapel at once became, and at the moment when Vasari wrote still
remained, the most frequented school of Florentine
art. Among a class so large, and so aware of the
dignity and worth of their profession as were the
artists of Florence, nothing connected with the brief
and memorable career of Masaccio is likely to have
been forgotten or confused. And in truth Vasari
does not make a single statement concerning these
Carmine frescoes, which is not for me fully confirmed by the evidence of my eyes. In Rome with
its ever-changing, ever-shifting population of artists,
hurried thither from every part of Italy, and from
beyond the Alps, what tradition could hope to sur-
vive? The name of the real artist would be forgotten soon, and as soon would the work be ascribed to
the greatest kindred painter. In Rome a work
by Masolino almost inevitably would be ascribed
to Masaccio. Vasari probably reported Roman
spurious tradition as accurately as he did the
genuine one of Florence.

So much for Vasari. And now for the evidence
of my eyes. Forty years ago, before any very close

analytical attention was being given to works of art, the difference between Masolino and Masaccio might not seem striking ; and even now, to the raw recruit, it is not easily perceptible. To the properly-trained eye, however, there can be no hesitation between the two masters ; for, despite formal resemblances, their styles are severely distinct. Masolino thinks much less of structure than Masaccio, much less of grandeur and high dignity, much less of well-ordered and well-filled arrangement. On the other hand he cares much more for beauty, for delicacy, for suavity, and for colour. Then his draperies, far from having the supreme functional value that his more illustrious pupil gave them, are still involved in the calligraphic meshes of his Giottesque predecessors. In brief, Masolino was a master of a transitional character, as were his more famous contemporaries, Gentile da Fabriano and Vittorio Pisanello. To the perceiving eye, how different is Masaccio ! In his very small paintings, no less than in his monumental frescoes, we behold a creator and worshipper of the heroic style. He disdains individual expression, cares little for beauty, is never tender, but always majestic, aloof, almost awe-inspiring. With this passion for the grandly essential, went a certain indifference to details. His hands, for instance, are not always irreproachable, and his ears are apt to be not at all parallel with the nose, but at an ugly angle to it. Trifling as this last detail may seem to the æsthetician, to us, as archæologists, it is, in this instance, of no small importance.

With these distinctions between master and pupil in mind, I cannot readily conceive how a properly-trained eye can fail to note how widely the " Raising of Tabitha " in the Brancacci Chapel departs from Masaccio's " Tribute Money " on the opposite wall.

[Church of the Carmine, Florence.

DETAIL FROM ST. PETER RAISING TABITHA

The one still has the bonelessness, the lack of proportions, the attitudes, the gestures, and the gaiety of the Transition and even of the Giottesque; while the other is of the ruggedness of the rocks, and of the massiveness of the mountains, monumental and grand to a degree that no art since then, not even Michelangelo's, has rivalled. A not unapt literary parallel would be the difference between the Book of Esther and the Book of Job. Of one who should say that Masaccio was not always thus, I would ask where he is not? Surely he is the same essentially, if in a slightly milder form, in the small *predelle*, and even in the Birth-plate at Berlin.

For me and the like of me in this instance, such evidence as this suffices so amply, that I will not give any of a morphological kind; although the more carefully you compare this "Raising of Tabitha" with the frescoes at Castiglione d'Olona, the stronger must grow your conviction that they are by the same hand.

At last we can return to our thesis, which is that a certain Madonna at Munich and a certain fresco at Empoli are both by Masolino.

The Munich Madonna sits on a cushion, looking tenderly but sadly at the Child, who throws up his little hands to her bare breast. On each side, kneeling on cloudlets, with wings outspread, we see two angels, and above, God the Father, appearing in the midst of cherubim, sending forth the Holy Spirit in the form of a dove.

This "Trinity" is catalogued in Munich as a Florentine work of about 1440. A late date this, surely, for a work of such transitional character. The Eternal is almost purely Giottesque; the Madonna's face would not be out of place at the end of the Trecento; her sitting upon a cushion points to

the same time ; and the folds of the draperies show
but little advance upon that epoch, although that
little is significant enough.   More decided Quattrocento feeling is confined to the angels, and to the
firmer modelling, particularly that of the Child.

Now had this panel really been painted twelve
years after Masaccio's death, at a time when Fra
Angelico already had the bulk of his work behind
him, we should have to assume that its author was one
of those uncouth *rétardataires* who take up with an
idea only when the more nimble wits are beginning
to leave it.   But such folk betray themselves in at
least two ways : either they are as crude in execution
as they are dull in spirit ; or they manifest exactly
contemporary influence somewhere ; or, indeed, they
do both.   In the panel before us, however, there is
no trace of Angelico's influence.   A hasty glance
might discover a likeness to that master in the
angels ; but careful inspection reveals the superfi-
ciality of this likeness.   What there is, is of the kind
due to contemporaneity rather than to imitation.
Had the author of this panel been an imitator of
Angelico, why should he have confined his imitation
to the draperies only of the angels ?   One surely
would have expected him to copy the faces, most of
all the Virgin's.   Nor was he crude in execution ;
for nothing could well be more dainty, gay and charming than is this " Trinity."   Note how carefully he
finishes all the extremities, how he has thought
out everything with regard to the draperies.   He
seems to realize that they should be functional, and
he makes them all that an artist could make them,
who has an as yet imperfect feeling for form and
structure, and habits of calligraphy that he cannot
quite shake off.   All this indicates an artist who was
pushing forward, struggling with the most advanced

THE MADONNA AND CHILD, WITH ANGELS

ideas of his age, and not one who took up these ideas after everyone else. We can safely set aside, therefore, the statement of the Munich catalogue regarding the date of this "Trinity." It must have been painted not in 1440, but some twenty years earlier.

And by whom? One who knows Masolino's paintings at Castiglione d'Olona as well as he knows the faces, the gestures, and the step of his most intimate friends—and only when he does so know a given master has the student a right to discuss what is attributed to him—one who thus knows Masolino, must recognize at a glance that he was the author of our "Trinity." It is so obvious that, for this very reason, attempting to demonstrate it seems as absurd, and really is as difficult, as to prove to people who never have seen him that such a person is such and such a friend of ours. Yet in this case the attempt must be made. The Madonna, then, has the aquiline type which we find repeatedly at Castiglione, particularly wherever faces are seen a little sideways. The angels are of the type of those there, especially of the one kneeling at St. Luke's feet. The Eternal is almost identical with the St. John in the "Baptism of Christ," or with the head on Christ's right in the "Baptist Preaching." As in those frescoes, the eyes tend to turn slightly upwards at the outer corners. The hair of the angels finds its parallel repeatedly, and so do the folds of the draperies. I invite especial comparison with those of the Evangelist.

There thus can be no reasonable doubt that Masolino was the author of this panel. No other name can be brought into connection with it at all, unless it be Masaccio's. And the student who will examine the latter's youthful work, the "Madonna with St. Anne" in the Florence Academy, or the

"Adoration of the Magi" at Berlin, another early work, will readily acknowledge that Masaccio started where Masolino left off, and that he, Masaccio, could not have been the author of the Munich panel. This finally is so like the "Madonna" at Bremen, as to leave no doubt that they are by the same hand. That work, however, is distinctly more advanced, and as it is dated 1423, we may safely assign the picture which we have been discussing to about 1420.

The fresco at Empoli was, until a year or two ago, almost invisible, being hidden by one of those baroque screens intended to enhance the holiness of sacred images. It is placed very high within a recessed arch. It is therefore extremely difficult to photograph, and our reproduction is, in consequence, far from satisfactory. Yet some idea of its delicacy, its refinement, its great beauty the reader will scarcely fail to get. The Madonna holds the Child against her left side, while two angels with arms folded over their breasts stand by, prayerfully and wistfully. The faces have the gentleness and loveliness that characterize Masolino. The Child is sturdy and full of solemn dignity as he blesses. He is not nude, but dressed in one of those embroidered robes which Masolino loved to paint. The colouring is of a radiant splendour, quite unparalleled elsewhere in Tuscan painting— due in part to the amazing preservation in which we find this work, but more still to Masolino's noted proficiency as a fresco painter. Listen to what Vasari says on this head : "But Masolino's greatest merit of all was in fresco painting. This he did so well, toning and harmonizing his colours with such refinement, that his flesh parts have the utmost delicacy that can be imagined."

MASOLINO

Empoli.

THE MADONNA AND ANGELS

This work again is so obviously Masolino's, that it seems useless to attempt to prove it. Yet for sceptics a few words by way of demonstration will scarcely be out of place. Let them, then, compare the head of this Virgin with that of the elegant youth seen full face in the " Raising of Tabitha," or that of the curly-headed youth in " Herod's Feast " at Castiglione. The same proportions, the same tender look in the eyes, the same sweet mouth, and the same shape of nose. Here as ever in Masolino, the outer corners of the eyes are turned slightly upward. The angels are of the exact type we already have encountered at Castiglione and in the Munich " Trinity."

But this fresco betrays considerable advance upon the last-named panel, and perhaps even on the Castiglione works. Masolino's feeling for form and dignity has greatly increased, and the Child is almost as rugged in build, and stern in expression, as if he had been painted by Masaccio. This master's name, however, should not be attached to this fresco. For him it is altogether too soft and delicate ; for him, the hands are too refined and too daintily finished ; for him, the colouring is too brilliant and transparent. Nor is there any antecedent improbability in Masolino's having worked at Empoli. He, if any one, must have found this town on his road, for his home at Panicale was at no great distance.

This, however, is not the only fresco that he left at Empoli. There in the Baptistery we see a " Pietà " of such depth of feeling combined with such noble restraint, that it reminds us of Bellini's greatest versions of this subject. It already has been noted by the " Cicerone," who ascribes it dubitatively to Masaccio, and by myself, who have with some hesitation attributed it to Masolino. I

have now cast away all doubt, and am convinced
that it is his. Masaccio's it certainly is not. Both
on panel and fresco his colouring was always darker
and more opaque than this, which has all the blond-
ness and brilliancy which we invariably find in
Masolino's frescoes. The types are those aquiline
ones which meet us constantly in his works where
faces are seen sideways. The Virgin is the one at
Munich grown old. Note also how she resembles a
turbanned man in the "Raising of Tabitha." For
Masaccio, the Christ has neither sufficient form nor
structure; but observe his likeness in these respects
to the Saviour in the "Baptism" at Castiglione,
and how much his face, although dignified by suffer-
ing, resembles that of Christ in the "Preaching of
the Baptist," also at Castiglione. How different
both from the more massive, less expressive Christ
in Masaccio's "Tribute Money!" Finally, I must
draw the reader's attention to the upper part of the
fresco. There, out of a round opening, appears a
prophet throwing up his hands in horror at what he
beholds. Where, in all of Masaccio's undisputed
works, shall you find so Trecento a type as this?
This type appears not seldom in Masolino. Twice
you see him, the exact type, and the self-same action
in the "Raising of Tabitha" alone. He resembles
the Eternal in the Munich panel. Slightly different,
you find him again and again at Castiglione, now as
Herod, then as an Evangelist, and again as the
Baptist.

Thus Empoli can rejoice in two works by Masolino, not the most considerable, but one the most
lovely, and the other the most noble, which, so far
as we know, he ever painted. But is there nothing
else of his in the neighbourhood? Close by, at
S. Miniato al Tedesco, in the Dominican Church,

A PIETÀ

[*Baptistery, Empoli.*

on the right as you enter the chapel to the right of the choir, there is the fragment of a fresco representing a deacon. In the Franciscan church there is a frescoed St. Christopher. Both are in a miserable state of ruin ; but originally they could scarcely have been strange to Masolino's art.

AN UNPUBLISHED MASTERPIECE BY FILIPPINO LIPPI

THE fame which for centuries surrounded Filippino Lippi's name, as one of the greatest masters of the Florentine School, is likely, as knowledge and taste advance, to diminish rather than to increase. Recent criticism has shorn him of a number of pictures traditionally attributed to him ; and among this number some of the most charming of all those that went under his name—such as the series of panels containing the story of Esther ; and although a great many indisputable works of his remain, they cannot seriously be compared in quality with those of his master Botticelli, or even of his father, Fra Filippo. No other painter who employed, as he did, the forms of the fifteenth century, departed so far from the artistic spirit of that epoch. He was, in fact, a precursor of the æsthetic confusion of the Seicento.[1] He had all its sentimentality, all its indiscriminate profusion of ornament, all its fondness for empty display. Like the painters of that later time, he

---

[1] *Seicentismo*, like any other movement which takes its name from a century, actually anticipated its nominal date by a generation or more. Thus, what we know as the spirit of the eighteenth century, or, again, as the spirit of the nineteenth century, was really in many respects more clearly manifest before the end of the century preceding. By *seicentismo*, therefore, one does not mean a style confined to the seventeenth century, but one that began long before, and culminated soon after, the beginning of that century.

[*Badia Church, Florence.*

THE APPEARANCE OF THE VIRGIN TO ST. BERNARD

had ceased to listen to the "still, small voice;" and, in his impatience to produce an effect, he forsook the simplicity of his contemporaries, and rushed into the *baroque*. He is akin rather to the family of Domenichino, than to the descendants of Masaccio.

To a certain degree, however, it is undeniable that Filippino is the victim of ill-luck. (I use the present tense with intention, for I am speaking of the personality of the artist, not of the man, and his artistic personality can never belong completely to the past, so long as the works which express it endure.) Of his first works, painted before the sketch-books he made in Rome provided him with the means to burst out as it were into the dubious opulence of a *nouveau riche*, some have entirely disappeared; others—like the admirable *tondo* of the Corsini Gallery at Florence—have remained relatively unknown ; and others still, his frescoes in the Brancacci Chapel, his most serious achievement perhaps, are crushed by the too close proximity of Masaccio.

To my feeling, Filippino Lippi's full value appears in only two pictures among those well known to the public—the " Vision of St. Bernard" in the Badia, and the " Madonna with the Donor, Tanai di Nerli," in S. Spirito, at Florence. His other well-known paintings belong to the province of the connoisseur, the archæologist, the explorer : these two works alone live, or should live, in the memory of everyone who cares for beauty ; for they are illuminated, if not with the splendour of genius (of which, in his case, there is hardly question), at least with the beneficent warmth which emanates, at its best moments, from a talent both delicate and suave.

To these two masterpieces I propose to add a third, which is not inferior to the " Vision," and

seems even finer than the " Madonna " of S. Spirito.
And just here we have an instance of Filippino's
bad luck. This picture which, if it were in the Uffizi
or any other famous public gallery, would certainly
add great lustre to the master's name, is in a private
collection in the United States.[1] The fortunate owner
of this masterpiece is Mrs. S. D. Warren of Boston.
Thanks to her kindness, I am able to offer to the
readers of this volume an excellent reproduction
of it.

It is a *tondo* with figures under life size. The
Virgin is seated in the foreground, beneath a
loggia, with a background of landscape containing
buildings and trees. The Child, whom she holds on
her knees, leans forward to embrace the little John,
who is held by St. Margaret. To the left is
St. Joseph leaning on his staff. A parapet in front
is strewn with a confusion of objects, a wicker basket,
a book, an elliptical wooden box, and the reed cross
which St. John has just laid down.

It would be difficult to find a more fascinating
composition. The figures are in perfect harmony
with the surrounding space : they neither lose themselves in stretches of sky and land too vast for them
to hold their own in, as the figures do in a number
of fifteenth-century pictures ; nor are they crowded
and stifled, as in the *tondi* of Signorelli, or the
" Madonna della Seggiola " of Raphael. The
Madonna dominates the whole. The other figures
only serve to complete the harmonious rhythm of
lines and contours, which give to the composition the
suggestion of a pyramidal silhouette that, inclosed in
a circle, never fails to produce an agreeable impression on the eye ; nor is the action less ably rendered.
We see Filippino here at the very happiest moment

---

[1] Formerly at Naples, in the Sant' Angelo collection.

FILIPPINO LIPPI

THE HOLY FAMILY

of his career, as far from the almost rigid im-
movability of his Virgin in the Uffizi altar-piece or
of the Madonna in the "Vision" of the Badia, or
even of the one in the Corsini *tondo*, as from the
aimless and nervous agitation of his last paintings.
Everything is gracious, measured, serene. Rarely
if ever has the Leonardesque *motif* of the two holy
children embracing each other, been rendered with
greater naturalness and freedom from affectation.
Worthy of note also is the way the right arms of the
female figures and the children are entwined, so as
to form a semicircle within the *tondo*. If Filippino
had been a Leonardo, their arms and hands would
have been drawn with more life, one would have
realized more vividly that they were organic and
prehensile members : if he had been Raphael, the
arrangement of line would doubtless have been more
simple and grand; but no one could have solved
such a difficult problem of composition with surer
taste than has been shown here by Filippino—and
taste is far from being the constant accompaniment
of his genius. The drawing, finally, is on a level
with the composition and the action. Certainly it is
not of the very first order; from Filippino we may
not expect either the line of Botticelli or the power
of Masaccio or Michelangelo. And yet the contours
are functional while refined ; the folds of the draperies
express clearly their purpose, the figures undeniably
have a life of their own. The colour is gay and
transparent, as in the Badia altar-piece. Nor must
we forget to mention the exquisite oval of the
Virgin's face, where an almost Raphaelesque grace
is enhanced by the noble severity of the Florentines.[1]

[1] In the Corsini Gallery at Rome, on the back of a study by
Filippino representing "St. Francis founding his Third Order,"
there is a head very close in type to the one before us.

A careful comparison of this *tondo* with the rest of Filippino's works makes me wonder whether one should not give it rank as his masterpiece—indeed, neither at the Badia nor in S. Spirito does he attain to such felicity in composition, and to such freedom from the faults, which betray the frailty of his charming talent. Although it is impossible to assign an exact date to this *tondo*, it is easy to fix the period of the master's career to which it belongs. Among all his works, the one with which it has most in common is the altar-piece in S. Spirito. Setting aside the general resemblances, which are too obvious to dwell upon, let us come to a more intimate analysis. In both pictures we feel the beginnings of the tendency to that style of baroque ornament which burst forth, later, in the frescoes of the Strozzi Chapel, and in almost all Filippino's subsequent works. The dwarfs who support the capital in this picture resemble the marine gods who surround the throne of the Virgin in S. Spirito. The decoration of the pillar is the same in both pictures. The left hand of the Virgin in the latter work is identical with that of St. Margaret here, and her right hand corresponds exactly with St. Catherine's in S. Spirito. Furthermore, both pictures give us, for the first time in Filippino's works, a landscape background filled with picturesque architecture of Northern style.

Signor Cavalcaselle was inclined to believe that Filippino painted the altar-piece of S. Spirito, before beginning the frescoes in S. Maria sopra Minerva at Rome, that is to say, immediately after having finished the Badia picture : in support of this view he cites the fresco of " St. Thomas before the Crucifix." [1] But I, for my part, find that the

[1] "Storia della Pittura italiana," vol. vii., p. 26.

THE VIRGIN AND CHILD WITH VARIOUS SAINTS

stylistic differences between the pictures of the Badia and S. Spirito, are too great to allow of his having begun the latter, as Cavalcaselle's hypothesis demands, immediately after finishing the former. Furthermore, one may reasonably doubt whether the interval of time between the termination of the Badia "Vision" and the commencement of the Minerva frescoes was really enough to permit him to carry through the execution of two masterpieces of such size as the S. Spirito altar-piece and Mrs. Warren's *tondo*. These two pictures are much too close in style for us to imagine that the one was painted *before*, and the other *after*, the Roman frescoes. The two panels, moreover, present characteristics which are not found in the frescoes, nor, *à fortiori*, in the earlier works. The pillars, for example, are decorated with panoplies, a detail which continually recurs in the Strozzi Chapel, and the other works Filippino carried out in his later years; while, even in the Minerva frescoes, the decoration is entirely of leaves and flowers, or of mere grotesques. I have said that the background of Northern architecture appears in Mrs. Warren's *tondo* for the first time; but the same background is found again and again in later works, not only in the Strozzi Chapel, but in works evidently of a very advanced period, such as the "Visitation" at Copenhagen, and the "Madonna" at Berlin (No. 101). Finally, the St. Margaret of our *tondo* is already of the delicate, frail, and slightly ailing, type that we find in that one of the Strozzi frescoes which is dated 1502, the "Resurrection of Drusiana."

From what has just been said, it would thus appear that these two pictures were painted after Filippino had finished the frescoes in S. Maria sopra Minerva; and directly after, before the master had seriously begun his work in the Strozzi Chapel. In 1496, when Filippino finished his " Epiphany," now in the Uffizi (No. 1257), it is clear that a picture like the Warren *tondo* already belonged to his past; on the other hand, because of its greater ease and freedom, and because of the anticipation of types that recur later, this work seems to me to have been painted after, not before, the one in S. Spirito. If these observations are well founded, the two magnificent panels we have been considering must have been painted about 1493 or 1494.

The presence in Mrs. Warren's *tondo* of St. Margaret, a figure rarely occurring in Florentine art, suggests the idea that if it were not actually painted for the convent at Prato dedicated to this saint— where, we remember, Filippino's mother, Lucrezia Buti, was once a nun—it was done on the order of some person or some family of Prato, who shared with the nuns of that town the cult of St. Margaret.

FILIPPINO LIPPI

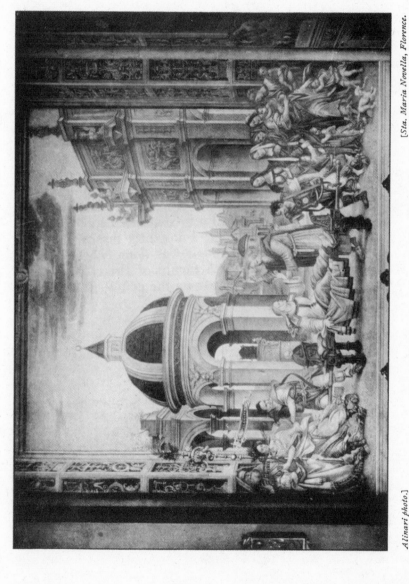

ST. JOHN THE BAPTIST RAISING DRUSIANA

AN ALTAR-PIECE BY GIROLAMO
DA CREMONA

In the good old days, when genius was in fashion, a
work of art, not authenticated by documents, was
invariably ascribed to the greatest master whose
style it was thought to resemble. And now that
some of us are beginning to return to the opinion,
certainly far more attractive and quite as tenable,
that in the work of art at least, genius is, after all,
everything,—now that we have made the complete
round, we meet at the opposite end the good folk
who are for the first time hearing of environment,
historical methods, importance of local phenomena,
and all the rest of the late M. Taine's well-known
views. The enigmatic work of art has suddenly
ceased to be a masterpiece by Leonardo or Michelangelo, Raphael or Giorgione, Mantegna or Giam-
bellini, and become a most interesting specimen by
the local painter whose name Signor So-and-So,
parish-inspector of antiquities, with the aid of
Canonico So-and-So, who has a turn for old parch-
ment, has unearthed as the indubitable author of a
faded and appalling fresco in the sacristy of the
parochial church.

Until the other day, a fascinating altar-piece in
the cathedral of Viterbo used to be pointed out to
you by a friendly canon as a most unquestionable
work by Andrea Mantegna. Now it is no longer by
Mantegna, but, of course,—how could it for so long

remain unrecognized ?—by the local genius, Lorenzo di Viterbo.

But the old-fashioned criticism had used its eyes better than the new, and, though wrong, was not at all so far wrong as the new. Lorenzo di Viterbo was indeed capable of painting a work in quality no less than this, but he happens to have had nothing to do with it. The altar-piece is in fact Mantegnesque.

And now let me describe the picture. On a low, round pedestal stands Christ blessing with one hand, while the other is held in protection over the portrait bust of an old bishop who appears in profile, as large as life, at the bottom of the altar-piece. To the right and left of Christ stand the Baptist and the Evangelist; and between them and Christ you see the figures of St. Leonard, and of a monastic saint whom I cannot identify. The upper part of the panel is decorated with a hanging lamp, chains of beads and balls, and fruit. Christ has a very high forehead, with bright auburn hair falling in curls down to his shoulders. A white mantle wraps him about, leaving visible his right shoulder, which is covered with a richly embroidered tunic. The Baptist has curly, reddish hair, and wears a red mantle over a tunic of mauve. The Evangelist has an aureole of yellow hair, wears a pink mantle and an embroidered tunic. The figures are over-tall, but hold themselves proudly. The faces have great beauty, even inspiration. The whites of the eyes are rather prominent and bluish. The general tone is very brilliant. On the pedestal there is an inscription which reads: SALVATOR MUNDI SALVA NOS. MCCCCLXXII.

The painter of this altar-piece, whoever he was, either enjoyed the acquaintance of the young Man-

CHRIST IN THE MIDST OF FOUR SAINTS

tegna, or shared in the latter's novitiate at Padua.
The picture clearly reveals that much.   To begin
with, the hanging lamp, beads, and fruit are a species
of decoration almost confined to the Padua-Ferrara-
Venetian painters usually termed "Squarcioneschi."
The figures are over-tall, as in the earlier work, at
least, of all those masters who felt the influence of
Jacopo Bellini.   The feeling for form is considerable,
but the artist shares in the mannerisms as well as in
the dryness of the Squarcioneschi.   Compare the legs
of the Baptist here, their absurdly curved knees, and
their calves, with the legs of Mantegna's Baptist in
his St. Zeno altar-piece at Verona (Alinari, 13543),
of Bonsignori's St. Christopher in his polyptych at
SS. Giovanni e Paolo in Venice (Alinari, 13699),
or of Bernardo Parenzano's figures in the picture of
the Doria Gallery in Rome, representing a saint
giving alms (Braun, Rome, 141).   You will not fail
to note the kind of resemblance which occurs among
kindred only.   The draperies have their own tale
to tell.   The heavily embroidered stuffs are treated
in a way to remind us of Gentile Bellini in his youth,
of the young Carpaccio, and, above all, of the gor-
geous Crivelli.   In general character, the folds have
the Squarcionesque pecularity of giving way to a passion for calligraphic flourishes, while studiously seek-
ing to reveal the forms underneath.   Even Mantegna's draperies, as a glance at his earliest works,
such as, for instance, the Eremitani frescoes, as well as
his latest, "The Triumph of Scipio" (at the National
Gallery), will persuade one, are at no time free from
this awkward compromise between pure form, on
the one hand, and, on the other, pure ornament.
In our painter, the contrast of the long, dry Squarcionesque form of the Christ, for example, clearly
manifested, and of the swathing, swirling, eddying

draperies which cover it, is so strong that there is no accounting for it except on the hypothesis that the author, even while painting an altar-piece, was held down by the habits of an art where calligraphy was more at home—by the habits of the illuminator.

The draperies are not the only feature in which, as it seems to me, the illuminator's hand betrays itself. The very bright tints, the brilliant tone, are indications, no less significant, of this art. I would go even farther, and say that the scheme of colour suggests close affinity with the school of Verona, and that something in the types, and even in the feeling, strengthens this suggestion.

A painter who was also an illuminator, showing clear marks of affinity with the schools of both Padua and Verona—of course it must be Liberale, who, as everybody knows, worked for years at a place so near Viterbo as Monte Oliveto Maggiore. Yes, indeed! And when you look closer, see how much of Liberale and his pupil Caroto the heads of Christ and of the Evangelist remind you, how singularly like Liberale's are the folds of the draperies, particularly of this same Evangelist. Then, how odd! but this very arrangement of the group occurs in a picture by Liberale—the altar-piece in San Fermo, at Verona. (It has been photographed by Lotze.) There you have St. Anthony standing on a round pedestal, to his right and left on either side a bishop, and between his shoulders and those of the bishops on either side the head of a saint. In fact, the identical composition.[1]

All this is very true, and it does in a wonderful

[1] The editor of the last edition of the "Cicerone" seems to have read this article only thus far, for I see that he, who had never before taken the slightest notice of this altar-piece, now ascribes it to Liberale.

way prove that the Viterbo altar-piece is by a North Italian akin to the masters of Padua and Verona; but Liberale, in spite of strong affinities to him, he was not. Liberale's ideals in art were never so serious; he never approached Mantegna so closely as does the figure of the Baptist in the picture before us. Not only in his intention, but in his feeling does Liberale seem to be different from the painter of the Viterbo altar-piece, who had a subtler sense of beauty, and a deeper feeling for the significance of his subject. I will not go to the length of declaring that as interpretation the Christ here is successful. To my knowledge there is no satisfactory representation of Christ. But the face in this picture has at least a power of appeal, a something refined, something far from the ordinary, an infinite capacity for ecstasy. It shows a serious attempt on the part of the artist to think out the problem of what the face of the Christ must be like. The other faces are scarcely less ecstatic and expressive. Then the donor is among the greatest achievements in portraiture up to that date. He reminds one of Fra Filippo's own portrait in the "Coronation of the Virgin," now in the Florence Academy; but the Viterbese bishop is a vastly superior presentation, both as form and feeling.

Now all this was out of Liberale's reach. And when we descend to more obvious considerations we are equally obliged to reject the attribution to Liberale. The forms are not his. We have here neither his characteristic hand nor his ear. The drapery bears a very strong resemblance to Liberale, but is far less jagged, pointed, and crisp. Moreover, the author of the Viterbo altar-piece had a greater mastery over line, to which he knew how to give something, at least, of Mantegna's, or even

Crivelli's inevitableness.   Liberale's line is always more or less slovenly.

As we now stand, then, the Viterbo altar-piece is neither by Mantegna nor by Liberale.   Its author was probably an illuminator who studied both at Padua and Verona.   As an artist he reveals a talent inferior certainly to Mantegna's, but not to Liberale's, and scarcely to the talent of any other of his contemporaries not of the first rank.   Perhaps he would stand least out of place alongside of—let me say— Ercole Roberti.   Clearly he was no Central Italian, and the attribution to Lorenzo di Viterbo is sheer nonsense.

So much the careful consideration of the picture has revealed to us; and there, but for one fortunate fact, we should stop.   This fact happens to be the existence of works by the same hand,—works this time perfectly authenticated with regard to authorship.   These are a large number of illuminations, most of which are now in the cathedral of Siena; their author is Girolamo da Cremona.

Of this artist almost nothing has hitherto been known.   It was believed that he was only an illuminator, and it is certain that he worked in Siena, off and on, from 1467 to 1475,[1] and that in 1472 he did some illuminations for Monte Oliveto Maggiore.[2]   That Girolamo was more than a mere illuminator was first suspected by Mr. William Rankin, who recognized his hand in a "Nativity" of the Jarves Collection (No. 55) at Yale College.[3] Unfortunately I am acquainted with this work in the photograph only, which Mr. Rankin was obliging enough to send me.   Judging from this,—and it

[1] Vasari, Le Monnier, vi. 182.
[2] Vasari, Sansoni, iv. 584.
[3] "American Journal of Archæology," First Series, x., p. 149.

THE VIRGIN AND CHILD WITH ST. JOSEPH

happens to be adequate,—Mr. Rankin's attribution is so satisfactory that for those who know Girolamo da Cremona, an attempt to prove that this interesting little picture was by him would be an attempt to prove the obvious. To others I recommend a comparison of the two "Nativities" found among the Sienese illuminations (Lombardi, 210, 219). This "Nativity," however, is too close to the miniatures to increase greatly our estimate of Girolamo da Cremona, or to enlarge our acquaintance with his artistic personality. The Viterbo altar-piece, on the other hand, is so majestic a work, reveals, as we have seen, a painter of such high talent, that if I can establish that Girolamo was its author, I shall have proved also that, beside being one of the greatest Italian illuminators, he holds his own among the worthier Italian painters.

To describe in detail Girolamo's miniatures is not to my purpose, but a few words regarding their style and peculiarities will certainly not be out of place here. They have of course the brilliancy of all illuminations, and something of the garishness peculiar to the Veronese craftsmen. As compared with Liberale's work, they betray no greater mastery over form, indeed a mastery at times not so complete, but greater interest in form as a problem. They show but a languid interest in *genre*; on the other hand, their author cared very much to get the utmost expression out of the various figures he tried to depict. I would refer to the "Christ weeping over Jerusalem" (Lombardi, 152), with its tenderness and pathos; to the two versions of the "Vision of Ezekiel," with their apocalyptic ecstasy (Lombardi, 146, 147); to the even more apocalyptic figure of the white-stoled angel with his mantle fluttering wildly about him as he stands on the rock, *tuba*

mirum spargens sonum ; or to such tenderer moods
as we see in the "Three Virgin Martyrs," or the
"Assumption of the Virgin" (Lombardi, 173). All in
all, a profounder personality, a subtler artist, reveals
himself here than in any of Liberale's miniatures.
That the estimate is so usually reversed, seems due
chiefly to the incubus of famous names and the
written word, both of which make it so hard to look
at anything whatever with one's own eyes, to feel
with one's own heart.

Girolamo's closest affinities, as we discover them
in these same illuminations, are with Liberale, and
in matters more essential, with Mantegna and the
Squarcioneschi. The latter relationship would, by
the way, account for his greater interest in form.
Look at the "Nativity" (Lombardi, 219). The
kneeling Virgin and the Child are not only Squarcionesque in general, but prove clearly that Girolamo
was acquainted with Mantegna's "Nativity" (in the
collection of A. R. Boughton Knight, Esq., Downton
Castle). The feeling for line, where it is at its best,
is strongly Mantegnesque, even Crivellesque, and
the landscape has an equally Squarcionesque character, modified somewhat, it is true, by the scale of
the illuminator's art.

The character of Girolamo da Cremona, then, as
deduced from his authenticated works, corresponds
to a remarkable degree with that of the painter of
the Viterbo altar-piece. His works and this picture
reveal an identical spirit, an identical purpose, and
an identical training. The difference is in the quality,
a difference such as there must be between illumination and serious painting,—but to this point I shall
return later. Nor is there anything in the outer cir-
cumstances of the Viterbo altar-piece that would
prevent its being by Girolamo. It is dated 1472,

THREE SAINTS

and in that year Girolamo left Siena for a while to
take Liberale's place at Monte Oliveto Maggiore.
The distance between this place and Viterbo, both
practically on the high road to Rome, is so slight,
that Girolamo could very well have gone from the
one to the other in a day.

Thus there is every probability that Girolamo da
Cremona was the author of the Viterbo picture.   It
now behoves us to see whether a minute examination of diverse significant peculiarities will turn this
strong probability into certainty.

Let us begin with the types in the picture, and
first of all with the head of Christ.   It is very tall,
with an exceptionally high forehead.   We find these
peculiarities strikingly exemplified in the illuminations, particularly where Christ is represented :
" Christ addressing the kneeling apostles " ; " Christ
healing a leper" (Lombardi, 216); "Christ exor-
cising the evil spirit from a Demoniac" (Lombardi,
197).   In all these there is not only great identity
in ideal and feeling, but in the peculiarities mentioned.
They occur elsewhere as well : for example, in one
of the " Three Virgin Martyrs " ; in a face seen
over Christ's shoulder in the " Marriage of Cana."
The other types are not so easily matched, but the
Baptist has a decided and aquiline nose, which was
a favourite of Girolamo's, and may be seen in many
of his illuminations.   To mention a few examples
taken at random : the apostle on the extreme right
in the "Ascension" (Lombardi, 193); an "Apostle
striding forward" (Lombardi, 206); "a Sacrifice
according to Jewish rite" (Lombardi, 204); the
" Descent of the Holy Spirit" (Lombardi, 214).

In the illuminations as well as in the picture
certain figures are out of all proportion tall.   Good
examples may be seen in the "Annunciation" (Lom-

bardi, 220); in the "Ascension" (Lombardi, 193);
in the "Angel of the Resurrection"; and in the
"Assumption" (Lombardi, 173).

A striking peculiarity in the picture is the drawing
of the legs, which exaggerates the mannerisms of all
the Squarcioneschi, and, in the figure of the Evangelist, throws them out of all relation to the figure.
We shall not fail to find this matched again and
again in the miniatures. But one or two examples
must suffice : the striding Apostle's right leg has the
identical curve ; an absurd instance is the Christ in
the "Healing of the Demoniac" (Lombardi, 197).

Characteristic to a degree even greater than any
of the peculiarities already mentioned, are the ears,
the hands, and the draperies. In the illuminations,
owing no doubt to the more calligraphic tendencies of
this art, the ear tends to have no marked character,
although in so far as it has it at all, the form agrees
with the ears in the picture. Let me refer to the
"Almsgiving" (Lombardi, 198) as an example. No
closer identity than exists between the ear of the
Donor in the Viterbo picture, and the ear of St.
Joseph in the Yale College "Nativity," could well
be. It is, moreover, so very peculiar that to the
student who knows just how to use such evidence,
the identity in authorship of these two works is put
beyond all doubt—and, as we have seen already, the
"Nativity" is too obviously by Girolamo da Cremona
to need demonstration.

The hands in the picture are badly drawn ; so are
they in the illuminations, and in both they have the
same shapes and the same faults. Christ blesses
with a gesture almost identical with the one in
"His blessing the wine at Cana" (Lombardi, 218).
Both His blessing and His protecting hands are
paralleled by the hands of God the Father in "Ezekiel's

THE ASCENSION

Vision" (Lombardi, 147). The right hand of the Evangelist, appearing from under his cloak, has the shape and movement of Christ's hand in the illumination representing him as addressing the kneeling Apostles. The most singular hand of all is St. Leonard's. It runs out into an endless toothpick where the little finger ought to be. Now, we frequently find in the miniatures approaches to this monstrosity, but I shall cite only one example,—one of perfect identity,—the left hand of St. Jerome in the illumination wherein we see this saint and St. Anthony conversing (Lombardi, 201). Now, a peculiarity so singular as this is not likely to occur in two different artists having in common so many other characteristics as have the authors of the Sienese illuminations and of the Viterbo picture. They must have been painted by the same person.

The most striking oddity in the Viterbo picture I still have to speak of—the draperies. They have already been described as swirling and eddying. On the figure of Christ they assume the fantastic shapes of blown glass, of vitreous eddies sucked into vitreous whirlpools. The draperies of the other figures tend to take the same shape, particularly on the figure of the Baptist. Those of the Evangelist, on the other hand, are more usual, more like Liberale's. Now we shall not find in Girolamo's illuminations draperies with quite the vitreous texture that they have in the picture, yet the resemblance is remarkably close. Look at the angel with the trumpet to which I already have referred several times. Look at his long tunic. Its folds swirl into eddies, and are sucked up or down into little whirlpools, very much as we have observed in the picture. In the "Three Virgin Martyrs," on the other hand, the figure on the right has draperies which even

exaggerate the vitreous, tormented effect of the
folds in the altar-piece. Perhaps the most striking
resemblance of all in this peculiarity will be found in
the mantle of Christ, where He is represented as
addressing the kneeling Apostles.

I would now point out one or two resemblances
between draperies of a less singular kind. All the
Squarcioneschi tended to make the stuffs worn by
their figures drag between the feet; but seldom, if
ever, in a painting, have I seen this tendency carried
to such an extreme as in the draperies of Christ in
the Viterbo picture. This extreme is paralleled, if
not surpassed, in Girolamo's miniature of the striding Apostle (Lombardi, 206). The Evangelist's
draperies catch on the leg in two or three places,
while clinging to the rest almost as close as tights.
This again is a Squarcionesque mannerism, but what
is so curious here in the Evangelist is that, beside
pulling on the leg and clinging to it, the drapery by
some miracle manages to blow free to the side.
Just this singularity we find again and again in
Girolamo's illuminations, and a good instance is
found in the "Two Apostles" (Lombardi, 212).
One more point of resemblance remains to be noted.
The Baptist's girdle is knotted and the ends left
hanging or caught up, exactly and precisely as in the
girdle of "King David" among Girolamo's illuminations (Lombardi, 194).

It may now be urged,—

"True, you have proved that the Viterbo altar-
piece is certainly by a North Italian miniaturist who
was also a painter. You are right in declaring that
this painter was not Liberale. You also have succeeded in establishing a singularly close resemblance
in spirit, style, and in all significant mannerisms
between the picture in question and Girolamo da

CHRIST CASTING OUT THE DEVIL FROM THE MAN POSSESSED

Cremona's illuminations. But," the objector will continue, "there surely remains a something not yet satisfactory."

A difference does, in fact, remain, a difference in quality, in artistic intention, yet by no means not to be bridged. Even in the miniatures the quality as an average is very high, and in the figure of the angel reaches the height of the picture. But surely, illumination was one thing and painting another. An artist who practised both, if talented, surely would have taken painting as a much more serious business, and having an altar-piece to do, would exert himself as he would rarely in the pettier art, manifesting a talent surprising to such as know him in this latter phase only. Let us take a case beyond denial. Liberale's miniatures are charming and delightful; but who would deny the gulf between them and such more serious works as his St. Sebastians in Milan and in Berlin, his "Pietà" at Munich, or his "Death of Dido" in London? Now there surely is no greater difference in quality between Girolamo's illuminations and the Viterbo picture.

An interesting question suggests itself. Between Girolamo da Cremona as revealed in his illuminations, and as further revealed in the fascinating splendour of the Viterbo altar-piece, and Liberale of Verona, there certainly must have existed a band of connection. One must have had an influence on the other. Now who was the giver, and who the receiver? That is a question the full answer to which we doubtless shall find in Dr. J. P. Richter's long-promised work on the painters of Verona. I would meanwhile say that it must be by no means taken for granted that Liberale necessarily was the giver.

In 1472, the date on Girolamo da Cremona's altar-piece at Viterbo, Liberale was only one and

twenty years old.   For at least six years he had
been in Tuscany.   He thus had left his Veronese
home when he was fifteen or little more.   His
miniatures reveal a sturdy, gifted personality ; but
no trace of direct intercourse with the Squarcioneschi
is visible.   How old Girolamo was at this same
date—1472—is to me, at least, unknown.   Judging
from the maturity of the work, I should suspect him
to have been nearer thirty than twenty—at all
events older than Liberale.   His intercourse with
the Squarcioneschi is patent and must have been
direct ; moreover, it seems to me that he was particularly impressed by Mantegna's frescoes in the
Eremitani at Padua, and by the same master's altar-
piece in St. Zeno's, at Verona.   As these were done
before 1460, and as these are the works Girolamo
retained most in his mind, it may indicate either that
leaving this region for Tuscany at so early a date, he
saw none of Mantegna's later works, or that, being at
the most sensitive age at about 1460, he was most
impressed by what he saw at that time.   Even on
this later hypothesis, Girolamo could not have been
born much later than, let us say, 1442,—which would
make him nearly ten years older than Liberale.

If Girolamo was so much older than Liberale, and
as an artist not inferior, and if he possessed the
valued Paduan science, which Liberale certainly had
not brought with him to Tuscany, then it is scarcely
possible to avoid the conclusion that Liberale owed
much to Girolamo da Cremona.

Lombardi photo.] [Cathedral, Siena.

THE ANGEL OF JUDGEMENT

RUDIMENTS OF CONNOISSEURSHIP

(A FRAGMENT)

THE materials for the historical study of art are of
three kinds :
1. Contemporary documents.
2. Tradition.
3. The works of art themselves.
These materials are not presented ready for use.
The student is confronted with a quantity of data
of every kind supposed to concern his subject, and
he cannot accept them all offhand as being of equal
value. Examination soon reveals that some of the
data offered are suspicious, some doubtful, and others
positively apocryphal. He is obliged, therefore,
before going further, to sift his materials, separating
them into two groups : one immediately and distinctly valuable for his studies ; the other not wholly
useless, but only of remote and indirect consequence.

The process of sifting is different in each of the
three kinds of materials dealt with by the student of
the history of art.

I

CONTEMPORARY DOCUMENTS—THE DOCUMENT IN ART

The contemporary document needs the least sifting. We need only consider its genuineness (forged
documents being by no means rare), its correct tran-
scription, and its value as information or evidence.

Only the last question is within the strict bounds of
the art student's province, the questions of genuineness and text being better dealt with by palæo-
graphists and philologists. Confining ourselves,
therefore, to the discussion of the document as information or evidence, we must note that the art
student's attitude toward a document is not quite the
same as that of the student of general history. To
the latter, every treaty or agreement, to take one
instance, that he can find, if connected with his subject, is of the greatest importance, even if it never
was carried out, and never intended to be, the mere
existence of a sketch for an agreement between con-
tending interests throwing a flood of light on the
issues at stake, and on the relative strength of the
belligerents or litigants at the moment. A corresponding document in art would have much smaller
value, or no value at all ; an agreement between an
employer and an artist, if accidentally not executed,
being interesting only in proportion as the artist is,
on other grounds, interesting ; and ridiculous, in fact,
almost inconceivable, if its execution had never been
seriously intended. As information, then, the value
of the document in art study depends on the question
whether the work of art it deals with was executed,
or on the vividness of our interest in the artist.
But how are we to know that a certain contract
for a picture was actually carried out ? "The existence," we are answered, "of a picture corresponding to the description given in the contract,
still occupying the place for which it originally was
intended, or that can be proved to have been there
once upon a time." But there are reasons for not
being satisfied with this answer. In the first place,
as the descriptions given in a contract are extremely
laconic, being as a rule limited to the names of the

saints to be represented in the picture, and as it is always possible that the contract we happen to possess, even when prepayments were already accepted by the artist, was not carried out, the description in the contract would answer quite as well to a picture eventually painted by another artist, the contract with whom happens to have been lost.   The document, therefore, cannot be taken as absolutely sufficient proof that a certain work of art answering to the description it gives is by the artist mentioned. The document helps to establish such a proof, but the proof is complete only when confirmed by connoisseurship—which we may roughly define at once as the comparison of works of art with a view to determining their reciprocal relationship. Moreover, even if we had every proof that the picture was executed as *per contract*, from contemporary descriptions speaking of it as being by the painter named in the contract, and describing it minutely, we could not take it for granted offhand that the picture now before us on the identical site, or traceable to it and answering precisely to the minute description given, is necessarily the identical picture.   The original may have been sold secretly, or in such a way that no account of the transaction remains, and replaced by a copy which, poor as it might be, would yet correspond to the minutest description given in any text, mere description being utterly incapable of touching the quality which distinguishes an original from an exact copy, good or bad.   In this case, also, the decision is ultimately left to connoisseurship.

The further consideration arises that the artist often left most of the work, if not the whole, to be executed by assistants, unless a special agreement was made that it was entirely or in its most important features, to be from his own hand, although even then he did not always adhere to the terms of his contract.

A good instance is furnished by the "Baptism" in S. Medardo, at Arcevia, ascribed to Signorelli. Crowe and Cavalcaselle dismiss this work as a feeble imitation of Luca by some pupil. The "Cicerone" praises the landscape and the *predelle*, but not the principal figures. Now, quite recently, the contract was published in which Signorelli undertakes to paint the three principal figures entirely with his own hand, leaving the rest to his best assistants; but the document changes nothing, it being incredible that Signorelli could possibly have sunk so low as to be responsible for the principal figures of this "Baptism," which are not from his own hand, in spite of the promise to execute them himself. Signorelli was not the only painter with a low sense of business honour. Titian was scarcely better. He sent out quantities of pictures as his own which he had scarcely touched, and comparatively early in his career one of his patrons, Frederic, Duke of Mantua, begs him to send works which have his touch as well as his signature. Raphael is another famous instance of a painter who did not hesitate to send out his assistants' works as his own, decorated with his own signature; it being an open secret even in his lifetime that such a picture as the "Madonna of Francis I." was executed by Giulio Romano. Often there could have been no pretence at execution on the great master's part. Everything painted in his shop was regarded as his work, even when wholly executed, and even designed by his assistants. No other explanation is possible for the number of pictures connoisseurship proves to be by Rondinelli, Bissolo, and Catena, all signed with the name,

although not with the autograph signature of Giovanni Bellini, proving that there could have been
no intention of fraud; and hundreds of further instances might be given, but enough has been said
to establish the point that the contract, the mere
document, cannot by itself perfectly determine the
authenticity of a picture, because it can never be
trusted to tell us just what parts were executed by
pupils.   That, too, must in the last resort be established by connoisseurship.

We have just noted that masters let their names
be put to works which they had not touched at all,
or but slightly.   This shakes our confidence in the
names that happen to be painted on the pictures
themselves, and leads us to a general consideration
of signatures and dates.

Signatures and dates require even more careful
criticism than other documents, because they have
been more attractive to the forger.   In some cases
fraud was clearly not intended, the owner taking the
liberty of labelling the picture with the name he
sincerely believed to be that one that would not be
discordant with the general character of the work.
In most cases, however, fraud of a commercial or
polemic kind inspired our forgers; and so frequently,
that it is by no means uncommon to find the name
of an artist on a work which is not even of his
school.   The name of a painter on a picture is not
without further consideration to be taken as an indication of its authorship.   Before the signature can
have any weight, we must carefully compare it with
all the other unquestionable signatures of the artist.
If it corresponds sufficiently with these, and is in
every way proved to be genuine, we are, even then,
not quite ready to accept the picture bearing it.

Connoisseurship must here also determine whether in morphological characteristics and quality it can be ranked with the already recognized works of the same artist. If it cannot, we decide that, although it once was doubtless a genuine work by the master, it is now too damaged to be counted among his still *existing* works.

To sum up : We have seen that in no case adduced is the document in art sufficient proof by itself of authenticity, or authorship. The document always needs to be confirmed by connoisseurship.

II

TRADITION

Having dealt with the criticism of the document, we now turn to a consideration of the value of tradition. The value of a tradition largely depends on its proximity in point of time and space to its subject. Say the subject is Eugène Delacroix : a tradition coming to notice for the first time now, in 1894, at Florence or Rome, is obviously less likely to be based on fact than a tradition going back nearer to his lifetime, and appearing in Paris, where he chiefly lived and worked. In the same way, a tradition about Giorgione that can be traced back to 1520, and to Venice, has more value than any tradition of later date, particularly if not traceable to Venice. There is, however, a difference in the nature of the traditions themselves. About Delacroix there may still be living tradition ; the memory, or at least memory of contact with the memory of his actual personal presence has not yet totally disappeared from Paris. But hundreds of years have elapsed since memory of personal contact with Giorgione has vanished from Venice. Except, therefore, in the case of masters of comparatively recent date, the term tradition practically signifies earliest writings about an artist. These, we assume, gather up all that was still remembered or known about a given artist, and the test of their value is the test we have already indicated—propinquity of time and place, to which must be added, the trustworthiness of the writer. Most of the traditions concerning the Italian art of the Renaissance are gathered together in three authors, Vasari, Lomazzo, and Ridolfi, dealing, for the most part, with the Florentines, the Milanese, and the Venetians respectively. Vasari's value differs in proportion as he is closer to Florence and to his own lifetime. Everything he tells us about the Florentine artists still living at the beginning of the sixteenth century has the value of living tradition, although allowance must be made for his occasionally becoming the mouthpiece of still smouldering hatreds, which make him a partizan even in matters of the past. His point of view, furthermore, is grossly provincial, not to say municipal, and his opinion as to the relative importance of Florentine art in general is not to be taken without criticism, and still less his estimates of artists such as Perugino, Pinturicchio, or Sodoma, who came from the outside to spoil the trade of Florentines and Tuscans. In such a case, also, as the rivalry between Raphael and Michelangelo, Vasari's statements must be taken with great caution. In the first place, Raphael had been dead many years when Vasari wrote, while Michelangelo was still alive, pleading his cause, and envenoming the minds of younger people against the rival of his youth; in the second place, Michelangelo was a Florentine, and Raphael an outsider; moreover, Michelangelo was Vasari's worshipped friend. This brings us to the consideration of Vasari's accounts and criticism of his own contemporaries. He means to tell the truth about them as he knows it—provided it suits his interests. If they were in any way his rivals, he did not hesitate to say the worst; if they were his friends, he said the very best he knew about them, and a little more. In short, his statements are never to be received without bearing in mind, on the one hand, his parochialism of spirit, and, on the other, the venality of his pen. These faults have less occasion for showing themselves when the artists he talks about are out of all rivalry with the Florentines in general, and with himself in particular, and his account of the Venetians is, on the whole, impartial as far as he is concerned; but as he had to acquire his knowledge of them for the most part at second hand, never having lived in Venice long enough to gather up the living traditions, he became himself again and again the victim of Venetian or Friulan parochialism and personal rivalries. As a source of information about the Venetians, therefore, Vasari is to be taken with the greatest caution, more even than in the case of the Tuscans. But unreliable as he may be, he is far more trustworthy than Ridolfi. Ridolfi, writing in the seventeenth century, after a complete revolution in ideals and methods, found no surviving traditions concerning the earlier Venetian masters than generally comes out of Vasari;[1] he has more to say about the artists nearer his own day, the old Titian, Tintoretto, and Veronese, whose descendants and followers he himself knew. Lomazzo need not detain us. His intention is not to tell the

[1] A tradition that, like Ridolfi's, can be traced to an earlier source has no independent value. Here, as in all historical criticism, the value of information is in proportion to the independence of its source.

story of the Milanese artists, but to write a panegyric
on the methods of the Milanese school.   His occasional anecdote can be taken only with the greatest
caution.   But granting even the perfect sincerity of
the tradition, we must always bear in mind that the
farther away it is in time and place from its subject,
the less is its value, and that in no case is it to be
pitted against documentary facts, or the scientific
deductions of the connoisseur.   Thus, Vasari sincerely believed, as all his contemporaries did, that
Andrea dal Castagno had murdered Domenico Veneziano.   There is now perfect evidence that Domenico
outlived Andrea.   Tradition is inevitably self-trans-
forming, mythopœic, endowed, while it lives at all,
with a momentum of its own.   Its final version of a
story, its final account of a character, is by no means
to be regarded as a merely idle tale.   In the event,
in the character themselves, are causes for the shape
they finally take in the popular mind, so that the
current version can be made to yield valuable results before we have wholly done with our studies.
But, in the first place, it is necessary to carefully
confine event or character to what it actually was.
Only then is it material fit for use in the first and
fundamental stages of the historical study of art.

III

THE WORKS OF ART

We have already mentioned the deductions of the
connoisseur as being of more value in every way
than mere tradition.   This point will be discussed
while considering the works of art themselves as
information, and evidence, in a word, as material
in the study of art.

In a sense, the works of art themselves are the

only materials of the student of the history of art. All that remains of an event in general history is the account of it in document or tradition; but in art, the work of art itself is the event, and the only adequate source of information about the event, any other information, particularly if of the merely literary kind, being utterly incapable of conveying an idea of the precise nature and value of the event in art.[1] An art that has failed to transmit its master-pieces to us is, as far as we are concerned, dead, or at the best a mere ghost of itself. Let us take Greek painting, for instance. We have considerable literary information concerning it, and a student acquainted with the texts, and at the same time with the practice of the art as a living thing, can make them yield many conclusions of a general kind as to the methods and skill of the Greek painters. But in so far as we have a definite idea at all, a visual image, let us say, of Greek painting, it is based not on texts, although helped out by them, but on our acquaintance with Greek marbles, bronzes, coins, vases, and scanty fragments of paintings, such as those of Pompeii, that have come down to us. It is the composite visual image derived from all these concrete examples that keeps us within the vague bounds of the Greek image-world, and prevents us from supplying with our own modern imagery the descriptions of Greek pictures that we read in Pliny, Lucian, or Pausanias. In that way we get a vague notion of what the great Greek pictures were like, and, vague as this notion is, yet, as we have seen, it never could have been supplied by texts alone. We have derived it mainly from those kindred arts which happen to have come down

[1] This arises from the fact that words are incapable of arousing in the reader's mind the precise visual image in the writer's.

to us, and without these we should not know even the very little about Greek painting that we know at present.

The text, therefore, or its equivalent in our studies, the document or tradition, is of value only in connection with the work of art; in other words, is not itself material for the art student, but material of great value in helping to prepare the real materials, the works of art themselves. The works of art themselves being the only adequate source of information in the study of art, everything depends on the choice made at the start of those which we consider necessary to the study of a given subject. Our problem, let us say, is the Venetian school: we wish to know how it originated, how it ripened to maturity, how it decayed, and what were its characteristics in all these phases. Our conclusions will obviously depend to a great extent on the pictures we have chosen to regard as belonging to the Venetian school. If we allow to slip into the number a quantity of Flemish, or Tuscan, or purely Byzantine works; if we pass unnoticed a quantity of masterpieces by the Bellini, Titian, and Tintoretto; if we disregard Crivelli and Lotto, and yet proceed deductively in our studies, our final idea of the life and character of the Venetian school is bound to be very different from the real one to be obtained by considering all the relevant factors concerned in the problem. As the factors in the problem given are pictures, it is of radical importance that each picture be submitted to the severest criticism before it is accepted.

Hitherto we have spoken of art in general, because what we have had to say applies equally to all the figurative arts. Henceforth we will confine ourselves more strictly to painting. Granting, then, the importance of testing each picture before we accept it as a factor in our problem, what is the nature of the test to be applied to it? We have seen that the document furnishes no adequate test, and mere tradition is of course even more powerless. We have already concluded that the adequate test is to be supplied by connoisseurship, which we have defined as the comparison of works of art with a view to determining their reciprocal relationships. It is now time to elaborate the definition, and to discuss the methods of the science.

Connoisseurship is based on the assumption that perfect identity of characteristics indicates identity of origin—an assumption, in its turn, based on the definition of characteristics as those features that distinguish one artist from another. A picture without signature or label of any sort is presented to us, and we are asked to determine its author. As a rule, the mere types of the faces, the compositions, the groupings, and the general tone, classify the picture at once as belonging to such and such a school. Closer examination of these features discovers a larger number of affinities with one particular following of the school than with any other, and the spirit and quality of the work reveal whether we have before us a great master or second- or third-rate painter. Our field of research is by this time reduced to very small compass, but the difficulties begin only here. Those striking resemblances which have guided us hitherto, become at this point not only valueless, but positively misleading. Types, general tone, and compositions a master has in common with his closest predecessors, his most kindred fellow-pupils, and his nearest followers, and they consequently cannot help us in distinguishing his work from theirs. We must leave them out of consideration in determining the precise authorship of a picture, and base our comparison on data affording a more intimate revelation of personality. We must begin by reversing the process we have been pursuing. Hitherto we have been eager to discover the closest affinities of the unknown picture we started with as an example, but having found these affinities, and having decided that the author of our picture must be one of a certain group of painters, we proceed to examine the differences between the work in question and the works of the different members of this group. Our attention this time drawn to the differences, we easily discover a number which lay unsuspected while we were searching for resemblances, and large enough to exclude as candidates for the authorship all but two or three of the group we had just now fixed upon. We then return to the search of resemblances between our unknown work and the works of the two or three candidates for its authorship, he to be adjudged the author with whose works ours has in common the greatest number of characteristics affording an intimate revelation of personality.

Obviously what distinguishes one artist from another are the characteristics he does not share with others. If, therefore, we isolate the precise characteristics distinguishing each artist, they must furnish a perfect test of the fitness or unfitness of the attribution of a given work to a certain master; identity of characteristics always indicating identity of authorship. Connoisseurship, then, proceeds, as scientific research always does, by the isolation of the characteristics of the known and their confrontation with the unknown. To isolate the characteristics of an artist, we take all his works of undoubted authenticity, and we proceed to discover those traits that invariably recur in them, but not in the works of other masters. Let us consider some of the questions we ask in searching for characteristics, and what answers we may be able to give them.

Of types, general tone, and composition we have already disposed, but very close examination of even these factors often reveals in the precise oval of the face, the precise cut of the features, the precise nuances of tone, the precise grouping and packing of the composition, characteristics of an individual kind, occurring in one painter, but not in another even close to him. These characteristics, are, however, so delicate, when of value, that the profit to be derived from their consideration is largely dependent on the personal equation, particularly as they may all, or nearly all, occur in a clever contemporary copy, itself distinguishable from an original only by inferiority of quality. The vehicle or medium rarely yields results, for two reasons. In the first place, in a school, and more particularly in a set or clique, these were practically identical; in the second place, most of the Italian pictures that have come down to us from the Renaissance have suffered from bad treatment of all sorts, and restorations. The very slight difference that there may once have been between one Italian painter's medium and another of the same close following are by this time as a rule obliterated. In so far, then, as considerations of vehicle yield results at all, they are not of the kind to help us distinguish painter from painter, but to place the painter in his precise school, and particular following.

Having disposed of types, general tone, composition, and technique, we are ready for the study of morphology, with the view of discovering what characteristics this study will yield. By morphology, by the way, we understand all that in a picture which can be distinguished from the feeling, or, as it is sometimes called, the spirit. The legitimacy of such a division is sufficiently questionable to suggest a fuller discussion of it than I can permit myself here ; but adopting it for the present as a matter of convenience, we must bear in mind that morphology includes not only the figures, and all that happens to be upon them in the way of clothing and ornaments, but the surroundings as well, furniture, buildings, and landscape. As it is impossible to put one's finger on certain morphological details, the execution of which is invariably different in every painter, we must have the patience to examine all the important details separately, with a view to discovering how likely each is to become a characteristic, bearing in mind, to start with, that the less necessary the detail in question is for purposes of obvious expression, the less consciously will it be executed, the more by rote, the more likely to become stereotyped, and therefore characteristic. We will begin with the human figure, considering important details from top to toe.

The cranium, as such, is almost never characteristic, chiefly because in Italian painting it does not always exist as a thing apart from the oval of the face, and in the cases where it does exist, is of too general a type, or too closely studied from the model to be the peculiar characteristic of a painter. Giorgione, Signorelli, and Leonardo are the most important Italian masters who give their figures a peculiar cranium—not that it always occurs in their figures, but we never meet it elsewhere, excepting of course in copies.[1]

[1] Several minor artists, such as Defendente De Ferrari or Amico Aspertini, have peculiarities, amounting almost to deformities, in

The treatment of the hair, on the contrary, is apt to be characteristic, because of its very nature. It is clearly impossible to reproduce every hair, and mere copying of the model is out of the question. The painter aims at a general effect, which he almost invariably attains in the same way, being the less hindered in his mannerism because the dressing of the hair is at all times very conventional. With different sitters, or for decorative motives, we may expect to find differences of colour in a painter's hair, and, to some extent, differences of dressing, but not differences of drawing, which, in this case, assumes almost a calligraphic character. One painter uses one quirk, or curve, or line, and another another, to obtain the same effect. They are, therefore, as characteristic as strokes, curves, and pothooks in writing, and would be of the greatest value if they were not capable of close imitation and copying. Minute examination will, however, reveal differences between the imitator and the master, although these differences being largely of quality, and almost wholly so in the case of the copyist, their value as a test must depend on consideration of quality of line.

The eyes are the most expressive feature of the face, and the painter is apt to make them the chief vehicles of his own intentions and emotions, and to subdue their entire look to his own purposes. The eye, therefore, is not at all so likely as the hair to be a peculiar characteristic. But what we call expression is itself the result of a combination of

the structure of the skull ; and Fra Filippo's broad, flattened type runs through his own works and those of his imitators. In giving any such instances, throughout this article, I do not wish it to be assumed that they are intended to exhaust the illustrations that could be gathered from the whole field of Italian art.

almost infinitesimal curves, lines, touches of colour, and spots of light and shadow, in themselves not at all expressive. The tendency is to form a habit of recombining them, and even in this case, where merely habitual recombination leads to the frustration of the purpose in view, which is expression, habit is apt to get the upper hand. The inferior painter has not the force to resist it; the self-expressive painter may have no desire to resist it, because habit in his case is apt to produce the precise recombinations that body forth his ideals; habit is resisted only by the painter with the power of isolating and registering phenomena, whose every work is, to the utmost degree of human capacity, a distinct creation. Even the eye, then, can be a peculiar characteristic, particularly in weak and emotional painters, and in reality there are very few masters who do not have some special trick of painting the eye. In some—to mention only the most obvious points—it is the way of drawing the line of the upper lid, in some the lashes, in others the lachrymal gland, or the outer corner, in others still, the lighting of the pupil, or of the surrounding parts of the face. In every case accurate observation only can tell us just what trick, if any, a certain painter has, but when discovered this trick is very valuable as evidence. The setting of the eyes, their relation to the nose, and their distance apart, although often very characteristic, as in Leonardo, Marco d'Oggiono, or Giorgione, are too easily imitated or copied to furnish a test of authenticity. Their value as tests, like that of all more general characteristics, is inversely as the probability that the supposed author attracted imitators and copyists. Of the three painters, for example, just mentioned, Giorgione and Leonardo each had a great following, and they were frequently copied, and by very clever copyists at that; while Oggiono had no following to speak of, and next to no copyists. Deep-set eyes in a picture point to Leonardo, as eyes remarkably wide apart point to Giorgione, but they do not establish any strong probability that we have before us Leonardo or Giorgione himself; on the other hand, eyes stuck on to the sides of the nose are an almost infallible test of Oggiono, as this trick is found in no other Italian master excepting, to a much slighter degree, in the Pseudo-Boccacino, who, like Oggiono, seldom, if ever, attracted copyists.

The nose, although not subject to a thousandth part of the variation for purposes of expression that the eyes are (such variation being possible only by means of the nostrils), is the feature which, more than any other, determines the character of the face, and all, therefore, that we have said about the eyes applies equally well to the nose, although not quite for the same reason. The weak, or self-expressive artist here, too, will fall into a habit of making the nose after a pattern; the observing artist will copy his model. Its mere shape is, however, in any case, of no value as a test of authenticity, because in order to reproduce the face at all, the copyist must carefully reproduce this most striking feature. But the ridge, the sides of the nose, and the nostrils, are peculiarly subject to play of light and shadow, and as the Italian painter was no profound observer of minute effects of light, he was apt to put on his light and shade in a conventional way, always, for instance, putting a high light on a certain spot. Even great observers like Titian and Moroni, so little the creatures of habit regarding most things, are conventional in the *chiaroscuro* of the nose. This convention being in every case the result of individual practice, is very characteristic, and therefore an excellent test—provided it has the touch of the master in question, that is to say, is an original, and not a good old copy.

The ears, although never alike in two individuals, do not, by their variety, except in cases of gross peculiarity, change the character of the face; and as they are incapable of variation for purposes of expression they attract little attention. It must be remembered, furthermore, that European man was very much less observant in the fifteenth and sixteenth centuries than he is now of things not immediately concerning his interests: of character and expression he was a keen observer, because they revealed to him how he must act to attain his ends; he was, as we know, sensitive to beauty of face and figure; but he was as good as blind to minute peculiarities that neither touched his feelings for beauty, nor concerned his interests. The ear seems never to have been noticed. What poet of the Renaissance indited a sonnet to his mistress's ear? The merest mention of the ear as a beautiful feature is so rare in Renaissance writers that it is hard to think of one instance, while, in our own times, the novelist rarely fails to tell us what sort of an ear his heroine had. This slight digression has been necessitated by the fact that, unobservant of the ear as most of us still are, we are yet startled when told that our ancestors as good as never noticed it. But just because they never noticed its character, nobody ever protested against the painter's giving it any shape, not grotesque, that he pleased. Having no inducement for resisting a habit, we do not resist it, and the Italian painter kept on through a lifetime painting the same ear, because there was absolutely no call for changing it. The ear is, therefore, neces-

sarily very characteristic of the painter, more characteristic, indeed, than any other detail of the human
figure. This arises not only from the fact that
he always painted it in the same way, but that this
way must necessarily have been a way of his own ;
the precise combinations of lines, curves, points of
light and shadow in an ear being, to all intents and
purposes, infinite, it is practically impossible for two
painters to hit upon the same combination.

But excellent a test of authenticity as the ear is,
its application is by no means easy, nor as proof is it
absolutely coercive. In the first place, we must be
able to distinguish precisely what is characteristic in
a given ear. If the ear were always an unchanging
outline nothing would be easier than to trace the
outline of one in a known picture by a master and see
whether it precisely corresponded to the outline of
an ear in a work of which we are trying to find the
author. But the number of cases in which the outline of the ear remains unchanging are too few to
permit this rough test. In most instances it is only
a part of the ear which is characteristic. In Botticelli, for example, it is the bulb-shaped upper curve ;
in Perugino, the bony lobe; in the Bellini, the cavity ;
in Lotto, the distinct notching of the line joining the
ear to the cheek ; in Moroni, the *chiaroscuro*. Only
training in the isolation of characteristics and careful study of all the known works of a master can
make the employment of this test profitable. Even
then, we must not accept its evidence unless the
mere trick also has the quality of the master, as, for
instance, the quality of line in Botticelli or Mantegna, or the quality of light in Moroni ; although,
as a matter of fact, the old copyist was apt to put
some characteristic of his own into an ear he copied,
or not to copy it at all, but give his own ear, and

this for the same reasons that he would not have copied the ears of his living model. The ear, therefore, when we have found its precise characteristics, furnishes a more valuable test than any we have yet discussed ; but it is conceivable that a master would have executed all that he thought important in a head, and let an assistant put on the ears. Rare though this practice may have been, the mere consideration of its possibility should prevent us from taking the ear *alone* as sufficient evidence of authorship.

No feature is so mobile as the mouth, and because we can move it at will, we have great control of its movements, and, still more, we can train it to take a desired shape when closed, or in repose. The mouth, therefore, affords not only an almost infallible revelation of temperament, but also of the degree of control in which the temperament is kept. But the consciousness of this tell-tale appearance of the mouth leads inevitably to the desire to shape it after the cut natural to the character particularly esteemed at a certain time. It is almost as correct to speak of the mouth in fashion in such and such a generation as of the dress in vogue at the same period. Now we must bear in mind that the painter of the Renaissance was still a mere artizan, in the sense that he was allowed as little to follow his own caprice in a picture, as a shoemaker in making a pair of shoes. If, in the case of a portrait, he did not give his sitter the fashionable mouth, he did not please ; if his other pictures did not have this mouth, they did not express the ideal of the day, and also failed to please. It was thus a question of fashionable mouth or failure, and so we are not surprised to find that mouths were apt to be painted in a stereotyped, and therefore habitual characteristic

way. But the very reasons that made it conventional, make against its becoming a characteristic peculiar to one person, as all noticeable
peculiarities would have displeased, and in the
smooth-lipped mouth the possible variations of line,
curve and light are not at all so numerous as in the
hair, or in the eye, and are thus less likely to contain
minute peculiarities. The mouth, then, as a rule, is
a better indication of the epoch and the school than
it is of the individual artist, particularly as it is very
easily imitated and copied, so much of its appearance
depending on mere rough drawing and modelling.
In a few cases, however, such as Botticelli or Perugino, the mouth is characteristic enough to furnish,
when it also has the master's quality, a good test.[1]

The chin, the jaws, the neck, are all too typical,
too easily copied, to be a ready indication of precise
authorship. Alvise Vivarini, for instance, has a very
full chin; Botticelli, very powerful jaws; Parmi-
gianino, a peculiarly long neck;[2] but the followers
and copyists of these masters share the same peculiarities, which can therefore serve only as indications of school, and not of the individual artist.

We have now considered every important detail of
the head and face, and we have found that they are
peculiarly characteristic in proportion

(*a*) as they are not vehicles of expression ;
(*b*) as they do not attract attention ;
(*c*) as they are not controlled by fashion ;
(*d*) as they allow the formation of habit in their
execution ;

---

[1] In no old master is the mouth so good a test of authenticity
as it is in Dante Gabriel Rossetti.

[2] None of these forms were ever so stereotyped among Italian
painters as they are in certain expressivists of to-day, *e.g.*, Burne-
Jones, Puvis de Chavannes.

(*e*) as they escape imitation and copying, either because of the minuteness of the peculiarity, or of the obscurity of the artist.

Having deduced these principles we are ready to apply them to all that remains of a formal nature in the work of art, and, in the first place, to the rest of the human figure. At the very start, we must obviously distinguish between the human figure nude, and the human figure draped—considerations of great importance in the one, arising scarcely at all in the other. Beginning with the nude, excluding all reference to antiquity, and confining ourselves chiefly to facts concerned with Italian art, and particularly with painting in the period between 1400 and 1600, we note that the nude, as such, was rarely, if ever, used as a vehicle of expression, for the simple reason that none of the public, and very few artists, were well acquainted with it, and therefore capable of understanding the meaning of its variations ; that it attracted no attention, for the same reasons, and, also for the same reasons, was not controlled by fashion. We should, therefore, expect to find that the nude would have been left to the caprice of the individual artist in those rare cases where he attempted it at all, and that consequently he would have formed habits of executing it. But the rarity of the attempt tended against the formation of peculiar, personal habits in the execution of the nude, and the nude, consequently, remained comparatively unchanged in an artist's hands from the nude as constructed by his master or masters. The nude can scarcely serve as a test of authenticity, therefore—except in the case of the great artists who created nudes of their own. But, even in this case, the test is to be applied with the utmost caution, as nothing so attracted copying and imitation as the nude, for the good reason that the inferior artist was next to incapable of creating a nude for himself; and as nothing is easier than to reproduce the mere outline of a nude figure, and its mere pose, the difference between the original and the counterfeit is largely confined to the quality. In the case of the nude, therefore, as in all the other cases we have been discussing, the ultimate test of the value of any touchstone is *Quality*.

The draped human figure is of course the nude human figure with clothes on, but it is only the great painter who exemplifies this obvious fact: the weaker painter nearly always makes drapery not so much what it ought to be, a covering of the nude, as a covering of his own ignorance and incompetence. The draped figure shares or should share with the nude, structure, movement, pose—everything, in short, except the drapery. The drapery, however, being so incomparably much more in evidence than the nude, absorbs a large part of the painter's attention, and requires special consideration; but before turning to it we have still to note a part of the human figure nearly always left as bare as the face, I mean the hands.

The hands, although in the draped figure they attract more attention than any other part, excepting the face, yet do not attract so much attention as any features of the face, excepting the ears, because the hands are not the rivals, in expression, of any of the features, and because, until comparatively recent times, they do not seem to have been regarded as indications of individual character. But their importance in the composition of the human figure draws far more attention to them, particularly to their colour, than to the ears. Thus we find, as early as the twelfth century, a heroine named after

her hands—Iseulte of the White Hands. Their
shape seems to have attracted as little notice as that
of the ears, and the artist was free to give them any
contours he pleased, and he nearly always fell into
a stereotyped or habitual way of forming them. All
that we have found applicable to the ear holds here
also; but we must bear in mind that, because the
hands attract more attention than the ears, they will
attract more copying and imitation, and that, consequently, they require even more careful consideration from the point of view of quality before they
are accepted as tests. In no case, however, can the
hands by themselves furnish a sufficient test. In
speaking of the ears, I said that it was always conceivable that a master would let an assistant put
them on, but in something so detached from the
face as are the hands, such a proceeding is a hundred-
fold more likely, and the absence of the master's
characteristic hand does not, therefore, inevitably
lead to the conclusion that he did not execute the
face and construct the figure.

It may be asked whether the hands are not even
more subject to fashion than the mouth, and whether
consequently the painter was not obliged to give
them the fashionable cut. The answer is that even
if the hands among the Italians had been a matter
of fashion, their execution permitted of such infinite
variety of recombination of lines, curves, touches of
colour, and light and shadow, that every master
could yet have formed habits of his own which
should escape the attention of all but careful observers. But I am not aware that among the
Italians of the Renaissance there was such a thing
as fashion in hands. Indeed, I doubt whether they
would have understood in this connection the words
" aristocratic " and " plebeian," which came about, I

fancy, through the fact that Van Dyke gave a certain form of hand to all his sitters. These were all of the upper classes, and of a time when aristocracy was already beginning to study itself with the object of discovering what distinguished it from the *bourgeoisie*, so as to furnish itself with arguments for its own superiority, and with tests to be applied to would-be intruders. The hand Van Dyke made aristocracy believe to be always characteristic of itself became a sort of social Palladium, and the struggle for its possession has scarcely ceased in our own day.[1]

We are now ready to return to the draperies, which, as we have already noted, play so great a part in Renaissance art because to its earlier generations the nude was unknown, and to the later only academically familiar. Man was then, as he has continued to be ever since, a clothed animal. His clothing is the most striking thing about him. As we walk in the street the first thing, as a rule, that we notice about people is the clothes they wear, and having made up our mind about them from this, we then look at the face, altering our judgment only when there happens to be a striking contrast between the person and the dress. Clothing being such an indication of the wearer, man has always been anxious to adopt the kind that would make him seem as capable of performing his function in life, and therefore as worthy of esteem, as the type supposed to have most chances of success. As this type constantly varies, dress also constantly varies, only very much more obviously and rapidly, the

---

[1] In the knees, the legs, and the feet also, when they are uncovered, it is not difficult to discover tell-tale peculiarities; but, as they are easily imitated, they do not, except in rare instances, furnish many minute tests of authenticity.

material undergoing change being in the case of dress so incomparably more capable of variation than the human type ; and dress is therefore *par excellence* the province of fashion.

Dress being so thoroughly subject to fashion, we expect to find the painter very much hampered in its treatment, and this always holds in the case of portraits, as far as the mere cut of the clothing goes. Outside the portrait, however, the painter, even now, is free to drape his figures as he pleases ; and it must be remembered that the portrait was late born, still rare in the first half, not common in the second half, of the fifteenth century, and of frequent occurrence only from the beginning of the sixteenth century. The Renaissance painter, engaged chiefly on religious, fanciful, or historical subjects, had therefore great freedom in the choice of draperies, and as this freedom was rarely restrained by structural considerations, it frequently amounted to licence, draperies becoming in the hands of many artists a matter of penmanship rather than painting. In such cases the formations of habit encountered no check, and we do, as a matter of fact, find that the less structural the artist, the more characteristic are his draperies apt to be. But even where the painter is perfectly structural, even when he is painting a portrait, and scrupulously reproducing the dress of the sitter, human patience is next to incapable of copying every fold that a certain texture will take in fitting this or that part of the figure. Sooner or later the painter is sure to grow weary, and to give the fold a turn that he knows it ought to take, or that he is accustomed to give it ; in either case permitting the intrusion of habitual and therefore characteristic touches. The recombinations in lines and curves possible in folds are far greater than even in the hair, and allow therefore of even greater freedom to the intrusion of mannerisms. The draperies consequently furnish an excellent test of authenticity; but we must bear in mind that in this case a painter may have, instead of one, a number of tricks in his draperies, each corresponding to a different part of the figure draped, a peculiar fold for the drapery inside the bend of the elbow, for instance, another fold or folds for the waist, another series still for the spreading of the draperies over the knees, and still again for spreading on the ground. All these draperies, nevertheless, are apt to have some small fold recurring in all of them, and when this happens to be, as it nearly always is, characteristic, it is in itself a good test of authenticity, as it is likely, by its minuteness, to have escaped the attention of copyists. The great number also of the combinations of lines and curves makes it even more highly improbable here, than in the case of the ear, that the copyist's or imitator's private habits would not reveal themselves on minute examination. But here, even more than elsewhere, we cannot afford to disregard quality. If the folds in a work supposed to be by a great linealist, for instance, lack in flow, softness, and continuity of line, no matter how the loops, catches, and curves are imitated, we may justly suspect its authenticity; in the work supposed, on the other hand, to be by a great structuralist, we can afford to allow that the line, as such, will have no very remarkable quality, but that it will itself be much more functional than in the case of the linealist, and that the arrangement of the draperies will be much more reasonable. As an all-sufficient test of authenticity, the draperies are, in any event, not to be considered, as they were so

frequently left to assistants : although their satisfactoriness, in a given work, tends greatly to establish
its authenticity, their lack of quality does not necessarily preclude the possibility that the master himself executed the more important parts of the same
work.

Before leaving the human figure, we ought to consider questions far more essential in connection with
a work of art than any we have yet touched—the
questions of structure, pose, and movement. But
structure, pose, and movement, just because they
are the body and the life of a work of art, are
eagerly imitated by those artists who have no constructive and life-giving talents of their own. All
that is in the nature of a pattern, therefore, all that
is merely superficial effect in the structure, pose, and
movement, is too apt to be imitated to furnish a test
of authenticity of any value. The essential, moreover, in structure and movement is the quality, and
this raises the consideration of these elements to an
entirely different level.

Continuing, meanwhile, our examination of formal
elements as tests of authenticity, now that we have
done with the human figure, we can turn to the
animals that the painters of the Renaissance habitually introduced into pictures, the horse, the dog, the
ox, the ass, and more rarely birds. They need not
long detain us, because in questions of detail all that
we have found to apply to the human figure can
easily be made to apply by the reader to the various
animals. I must, however, remind him that animals
were rarely petted, and therefore rarely observed in
the Renaissance. Vasari, for instance, gets into a
fury of contempt when describing Sodoma's devotion
to pet birds and horses. The painter, therefore,
rarely felt impelled to change the horse or dog he

had learned to paint, and his horse or dog was apt to be his master's, with more or less life to it. The differences are qualitative rather than merely formal. Let us take, for instance, a number of drawings of horses, mules, dogs, and birds indiscriminately ascribed to Pisanello. The types, the superficial appearances of the structure and movement, are nearly identical. The differences are wholly differences of quality. In the genuine drawings we shall find grace and rhythmical movement, spirit, life, an exquisite touch in the execution; in the other, these qualities will be lacking altogether in essentials, and largely even in minor points. But very rarely is the mere type so peculiar as to form a test of authenticity. Indeed, I make this category to fit into it at the very utmost three or four artists. Leonardo's horse has to my knowledge, particularly in the structure of the head, never been so imitated as to have the least chance of puzzling a scientific student of this master, and the same holds, although not quite to the same degree, of the horses' heads in Botticelli. Paolo Uccello's snub-nosed quadrupeds are also peculiar to him, and Carpaccio's strange hybrids belong to no one else.

Passing from the animals to the architecture, we are brought in contact with an element which can yield us scarcely any tests whatever of authenticity, because it is obviously more easily imitated and copied than any other, and because it allows of less differences in quality, so much of it being drawn with rule and compass. A very minute examination of decorative details may reveal points of difference between one artist and another of the same school, but those points would themselves be of a kind in which the copyist would find comparatively little difficulty in attaining to as much quality as the artist himself could put into it. All this arises from the fact that architecture is an art almost as capable of notation as music, and that an architectural idea, no matter how great, once registered is almost as easily copied as a sheet of music.

But I have already dwelt on this point longer than my subject demands, and interesting as are the considerations opened out, we must pass to the question of landscape as a possible test of authenticity. Plato in "Critias" speaks of landscape as something outside the domain of human knowledge; that the merest sketch therefore suffices, and the barest likeness satisfies, as nobody knows enough to criticise it. Although Hadrian, in all probability, would have found this statement incomplete, Marsilio Ficino when, in the middle of the fifteenth century, he first read this text, would have discovered, if he had stopped to think, that it applied to him exactly. Leonardo reports that Botticelli considered that quite a good enough landscape could be produced by a wet sponge thrown against a wall. And no wonder; for if man, in the fifteenth century, had not yet formed habits of observing carefully his nearest neighbour's less expressive and characteristic features, he was not likely to have given attention to what concerned him even less, the characteristics of landscape. Anything that could pass for rocks, trees, hills, and mountains sufficed; and, even later, when more was expected, portrait landscape was rarely required. The painter was free to give any landscape he pleased, and therefore tended to repeat again and again the same, or elements of the same. The landscape is, in consequence, a far greater indication of authenticity than we nowadays should expect to find it. Indeed, to such an extent is it characteristic of the individual artist, that even when he was exactly copying a picture of someone else, he did not hesitate, when the landscape was not too obvious a part of the work, to substitute his own. Witness the copies by Solario and Cesare Magni of Leonardo's " Last Supper," now exposed side by side with the original. Still, as the copying of landscape was by no means impossible, and actually occurs frequently, we must not take landscape even as a sufficient test by itself. Here, too, we must consider quality far more than the mere design, and must not lose sight of the fact that there was nothing to hinder a master who had himself painted the figures from letting his assistants put in the landscape.

We have now considered all those important formal elements of a picture which commonly elude the copyist or imitator, excepting the colour and chiaroscuro. Of the colour scheme, as a whole, nothing need be said here, because it is nearly identical with the general tone, which we decided at the very beginning of this essay was too typical, because too obviously imitable to furnish a test of authenticity. Other considerations militate against the ready use of certain definite colours as tests. In the first place, pictures are apt to be rubbed, scraped, repainted, or at the least encrusted with opaque varnish, darkened by the action of time, or merely dirty : it is therefore by no means to be taken for granted that the colour as we now see it is the precise shade the painter left on the picture. Then, even if we could make perfectly sure that a certain colour was the original, or at any rate the original colour affected by nothing more than the action of time (a change that therefore would have come uniformly, or practically uni-

formly, over the same shade in all the pictures by
the same painter)—even if we could be sure of
this, yet it is so very difficult to have a perfect remembrance of a precise shade, that unless we can
view a number of paintings by the same master
almost simultaneously, nay almost in the same act of
vision, we can neither be certain that the colour we are
looking at is particularly characteristic of the master,
nor, if already known to be characteristic, that it is
identical in shade with the colour in a given picture.
But despite all the difficulties in the way, the colour
test is not to be neglected, and with careful training
of the eye, in the isolation of shades, and in the re-
cognition of their identity in different lights, and with
training of the memory in retaining these shades,
the student may be able to make highly profitable
use of them ; for, although nothing so attracts copying
as colour, yet the imitation of the precise shade is
very difficult, and, as a matter of fact, never so successful as to puzzle the competent inquirer.

We have still to touch on *chiaroscuro* as a test.
Before we can apply it at all, we must, as in the case
of the colour, make sure that the picture before us
is the picture precisely or nearly as the master left
it. Even then, we must bear in mind that any
general scheme of light and shade, before light and
shade were well understood, was as rarely and
timidly used as the nude, and that later their broad
effects, depending largely on the lighting of the
studios, were not necessarily characteristic of any
one individual painter. That there are great differences need scarcely be said, but they are qualitative
rather than formal, while the broad effects are too
easily imitated to serve as more than the sort of
general indication of direction that composition, for

example, affords. On light and shade in connection with the various features of the face we have already touched while discussing the features themselves as tests.

Having now discussed for their value as tests the more important formal elements of a picture,[1] we are ready to look back and see what results we have obtained. We note that all the elements are easily divisible into three classes, in view of their immediate application as tests.

The most applicable : The ears, the hands, the folds, the landscape.

The less applicable : The hair, the eyes, the nose, the mouth.

The least applicable : The cranium, the chin, the structure and the movement in the human figure, the architecture, the colour, and the chiaroscuro.

Although we have found that the quality can never be left out of consideration—indeed, that it is always the highest consideration—yet we note in the classification just made that on the whole the ratio of immediate applicability of a test is inversely as the importance of allowing for the question of quality : the more important the question, the less applicable ; the less important, the more applicable the test. But we have also found that even in the most applicable test it is the qualitative rather than the formal element that gives them their value. The ears, the hands, the folds, the landscape are never to be applied mechanically, as if machine-made, and capable of being induced to coincide by superposition. If two leaves on the same tree are

---

[1] As a matter of fact, there is *no* detail, however slight, that may not be valuable as a test, but it is scarcely necessary to do more than indicate them, as I have done, in a summary way.

not absolutely identical, we need not expect absolute identity in two ears, two hands, or even less in two landscapes. The identity, it must be remembered, is in the visualization and habits of the artists, and it is there we ultimately must look for it. Rather than ask, " Is this Leonardo's ear or hand?" we should ask, " Is this the ear or hand Leonardo, with his habits of visualization and execution, would have painted?"

The forms employed as tests being themselves the resultants of habits of visualization and execution, the forms must inevitably change as the habits change. Habits, as we know, cannot remain stationary. Unless they encounter a resistance proportioned to their force, they tend by the inevitable necessity of mechanical laws to dig deeper and easier channels for themselves. The subject really demands a separate and exhaustive discussion, but at this point it is enough to indicate it as the cause of the inevitable though almost imperceptible change that constantly takes place in the forms of a given artist.

In the case of a long-lived artist, the forms in the works of his old age will scarcely bear a resemblance to those in his early pictures. It would never do to apply a test mechanically, even if a mechanical test were possible, without reference to the different periods of a master's career. A hand, an ear, a fold, a landscape background, that would be perfect tests of an early Titian, would, for example, furnish no tests whatever for a late Titian. As a matter of fact, every test has its time limit, and its application regardless of this limit, far from advancing the study of art, can lead only to a confusion which, in one respect, is even a degeneration from the chaos which reigned at the beginning of this century, when the connoisseur in the presence of a work of art rarely was satisfied with saying " This is a certain master," but always added "in his first, or second, or third manner." He at least took cognizance of the inevitable changes in style, and although we are amused at his sharp divisions into manners, as at the old historian's divisions of history into ancient, mediæval, and modern, yet his method was fundamentally more scientific than that of those students of to-day who apply tests regardless of time limits. Although the forms are, as I have already said, in a state of constant change, this change becomes distinctly noticeable only after a certain lapse of time. The length of this period varies greatly in different artists : in some it is five, in some it is ten, in others fifteen, twenty, or even twenty-five years. As, in order to ascertain accurately the authorship of a given unknown work of art, we have hitherto felt obliged to isolate its characteristics, and to see with what known works it has them in common, so, to make perfectly certain of the authenticity of a work, we must be able to say with which one in particular of the known works there is the closest community of characteristics.

Every test we have thus far discussed has, when satisfactory, a tendency to determine the authorship of a work of art. The question may, therefore, be asked : at what point shall we have a number of tests, each one tending to determine the authorship of a work of art, sufficient to make us feel that we have determined it ? This point, it can be answered, must vary with the presumable author. If he be one with a definite character subject to no violent change, if he be at the same time a master with

a distinct quality, we can scarcely be justified in
identifying a picture as his, unless we find in it practically all the characteristics of some one period of
his career.   If the author, on the other hand, have
no distinct quality of his own, no distinct character,
but be one of those secondary or even third-rate
artists whose career is chiefly parasitical or retailing,
we may be satisfied with comparatively few tests, and
be all the more satisfied with these, as such artists
rarely invite imitation, and as qualitative considerations need scarcely be applied to their works.   Thus
one, or two, or at the utmost three, very peculiar
tricks suffice to make it almost certain that a
picture of a Venetian or Lombardo-Venetian character of a certain epoch is by Bartolommeo Veneto :
this artist having no definite character, no organic
development, not even a type of his own ; changing with every wind, and never of more than
mediocre quality ; but possessed of a few tricks and
mannerisms sufficiently constant to enable us to
identify him.   On the contrary, no quantity of tricks,
mannerisms, and mechanical tests suffice to persuade
us that a certain picture is by Titian, because all of
these might conceivably exist in a forgery—all ready
tests in such a case being merely aids to the more
essential consideration of the question of quality,
which question increases, of course, in importance
with the importance of the artist.   Indeed, it may be
laid down as a principle, that *the value of those
tests which come nearest to being mechanical is inversely as the greatness of the artist.   The greater
the artist, the more weight falls on the question of
quality in the consideration of a work attributed to
him.*   The Sense of Quality is indubitably the most
essential equipment of a would-be connoisseur.   It
is the touchstone of all his laboriously collected

documentary and historical evidences of all the possible morphological tests he may be able to bring to bear upon the work of art. But the discussion of Quality belongs to another region than that of science. It is not concerned with the tests of authenticity which have been the object of our present study; it does not fall under the category of demonstrable things. Our task, for the present, has limited itself to the consideration of the formal and more or less measurable elements in pictures with which the Science of connoisseurship must reckon. We have not touched upon the Art of connoisseurship.

Index

INDEX